Interdependent Capitalism

Redesigning the Social Contract
through Inclusive Stakeholding

Interdependent
Capitalism

Joon Yun
Jeremy Yun
Conrad Yun

Published by

Yun Family Foundation

We are grateful for contributions from
Sung Hee Yun, Amanda Yun, Eric Yun, and Kimberly Bazar
&
Special thanks to Philip Auerswald and Dody Riggs

Contents

Prologue

There's no place like gohyang.

Perhaps no Korean word evokes a more sentimental response in our family than the word gohyang. It could come up in a spoken sentence or in a folk song. The term brings a knowing smile to my (Jeremy's) Uncle Conrad's countenance and prompts a faraway look from my grandfather. In English the word translates roughly to "hometown." In the Merriam-Webster dictionary, "hometown" further translates to "a place where one was born or grew up." No doubt it's a concept that triggers nostalgia for many Americans, although the word is relatively new to English, having been coined in 1879.[1]

To find a version of the word that evokes a resonance similar to the word gohyang, one must trace back to antiquity and the Latin word patria. According to Johan Huizinga,[2] however, by the time it appeared in the Old Testament, even patria no longer carried the full resonance of the ancient Roman word. It had become an administrative term about location without a great deal of emotional value.

For my Uncle Conrad and grandfather, gohyang evinces a sense of tenderness that exceeds even their own longing for a bygone time and place; it bespeaks of some sacred sanctuary, not unlike a mother's womb, belonging to all of humanity. My grandfather equates it with concepts such as heritage, lineage, and family in the deepest and most enduring sense. My Uncle Conrad attempts to render it in terms of metaphors: the place of grace where he wants to be buried; the timeless place that embraces you even after being disgraced; the place of eternal sunshine.

---

1. See https://books.google.com/ngrams/graph?content=hometown&year_start=1600&year_end=2000; Use of the word "hometown" is relatively new. It speaks to humans' increased mobility and coincides with the dramatic increase in life spans. People now lived long enough and were mobile enough to move away from where they were born.
2. See https://books.google.com/books?id=ge7_AwAAQBAJ&pg=PT105.

In the end, they agree when they refer to it simply as "home."

Once upon a time, "home" was our kin village. There was mom, dad, siblings, grandparents, and even our cousins, aunts, and uncles. We took care of each other largely according to our degree of genetic relatedness—what evolutionary biologists call "inclusive fitness." We were fed, informed, and governed by those who had our best interests at heart.

As human mobility and interconnectedness increased, our social dynamics changed too. Energy increases the entropy of systems, and human social systems are no different: whereas most humans were once frozen in one geographical space for an entire lifetime, we now bounce all over the globe. The diaspora that began in humanity's cradle has resulted in a once-inconceivable expansion of our lives and capabilities that drives an astonishingly positive discontinuity in the history of the human species.

However, this mobility has not come without a cost. Over the millennia, the strong, stable bonds of our kin tribes were replaced with weaker, transactional interactions among strangers. Where others have rightly focused on the upsides of our evolution beyond the kin tribe, we highlight the less-appreciated but foundational rupture that it caused.

Increasingly, the nuclear family has replaced the kin tribe as the integral social institution organized around inclusive fitness: nuclear families, closely related to each other within the household, live in communities of other nuclear families where the genetic relatedness between households is low. This shift—from social systems in which members in a community have a high degree of genetic relatedness to those in which members have little genetic relatedness—has fundamentally changed the day-to-day calculus of social interactions. Strangers have an incentive to put their own interests ahead of others', regardless of what pledges they may have made or oaths they may have taken to do otherwise. In short, our biological evolution has not kept pace with our cultural evolution. Over and over we expect strangers to act like they are our kin, and over and over we are disappointed when they do not.

For thousands of years, we as a species have been managing the tension between the social progress that occurs when we live and work in ever larger groups (from tribes to villages, to towns, to cities, to nations, and, ultimately, to today's globally interconnected cyberspace) and the vulnerability and disappointment that occur when we try to replace our lost sense of the ancestral home and tribe with institutional innovations. The empire, the church, the nation, and the corporation are all examples of institutions we have created to replace some or all of the functions of kin tribes. Each in its own distinct way has helped to advance our well-being as a species while also failing to deliver on its highest promise: the ability to develop a system of vested interest in others to replace kin-based inclusive fitness as the essential social contract. We have become so accustomed to this abuse of trust that we consider it to be nearly inevitable. In this book, we argue that it is anything but that.

When those entrusted to serve us are not truly aligned with our interests and don't have kin skin in the game, unfortunate things happen. A doctor chooses the most profitable procedure over the one most likely to benefit a patient. A politician betrays the public trust by favoring a well-financed special interest. A corporate board puts its own interests above those of the shareholders and employees.

The story we're telling is simple: family values have not scaled well as we have globalized. Not so many lifetimes ago, the heroes we admired were our aunts and uncles. Today, while the nuclear family persists, the roles of extended kin—such as that of my Uncle Conrad—have been reduced and displaced by strangers. Now we admire celebrities who maximize their own gains by encouraging us to buy the products they endorse. We admire "public intellectuals" who face no consequences when their consultancies and prognostications unravel into calamity. Such transactional dynamics have transformed virtually every type of human relationship, right down to romance being increasingly displaced by a quick hook-up culture.

When misaligned interests are combined with competition, a "race to the bottom line" ensues. If we force one media company to use less clickbait, another will use more in order to pick up the other's market share. If we force one food company to use less sugar, another will use more to fill the void in the market. In a way, the Kardashians and high-fructose corn syrup are really the same phenomenon—the inevitable outcome of a race to the bottom line, when misalignment meets capitalism. As for government, what started as a system of checks and balances has turned into competing checks written to the account balances of politicians.

Simply put, the time has come for a revolution in our social contract.

Due to evolutionary displacement, our social brains, which were wired for a high-alignment world, have been rendered maladaptive in today's low-alignment context. While reprogramming the underlying genetic source code may be possible one day, adaptation for now will have to be externally, culturally, and technologically driven, as biological adaptation will only proceed at its default, glacial pace.

Unless addressed, this evolutionary lag error between our biological factory settings tuned to the prehistoric era and the realities of the modern environment will continue to incentivize abusive behaviors. In this context, the so-called enlightened self-interest will promote further mutual misappropriation for asymmetric gains. The recent entry of computing algorithms tuned to bait and exploit human bioalgorithms could accelerate the mining of this evolutionary lag error by self-dealing social, political, and economic institutions.

In many ways those fears are warranted. Highly capable robots and artificial intelligence algorithms can subvert existing human neural algorithms for other uses besides serving human interest. Imagine, instead, building a robot of unconditional love—codename "mom" robot—to serve humans. Robots' algorithmic incentives can be designed to mimic the kin altruism of "mom."

Only through the development of such coordinated skin in the game among stakeholders, inclusively implemented, does enlightened self-interest produce the kind of great society envisioned by philosophers. In our view, encoding inclusive stakeholding into the new human social contract (i.e., creating new social DNA) to mimic the inclusive fitness of our tribal past is not just an opportunity.

It is a necessity.

———————————

My Father Joon, my Uncle Conrad, and I—co-authors who represent two generations of a family kin tribe—are writing this book to help audiences around the world imagine entirely new types of social, political, and economic institutions based on inclusive stakeholding, congruent goals, and a vested interest in the success of others—attributes that were inherent in the inclusive fitness of our prehistoric social systems.

Imagine the possibilities. Can we truly and authentically tie the success of teachers to that of their pupils? Can we tie the success of health insurance, food, and media companies—of any industry—to that of the customers they serve? Can we tie the success of elected officials to that of their constituents? Can we find ways to include other stakeholders, such as future generations and the environment and those who have no voice?

We envision the emergence of many models that will enable inclusive stakeholding in the way inclusive fitness powered the evolution of social systems. Of all the compelling possibilities, one stands above all: Interdependent Capitalism. The conversation will drive toward that point as the book proceeds.

Buckminster Fuller wrote, "You never change things by fighting the existing reality. To change something, build a new model that makes the existing model obsolete."[3]

We believe that rewiring human incentives around a vested interest in others by designing social algorithms for inclusive stakeholding that mimic the bioalgorithms of inclusive fitness will be the key innovation to create a better world.

———————————

3. See https://www.amazon.com/Fuller-View-Buckminster-Fullers-Abundance/dp/1611250099.

Whereas misalignment with competition is a race to the bottom line, alignment with competition is a race to the top. Imagine a world in which history, instead of being written by the victors, is made by helping others win. If we succeed, our transformative journey from the kin tribe to the interconnected global village will be complete.

This book is about how we will write that story together.

PART I

How We Got to Now

CHAPTER ONE

Kin Tribe

Many of us who live in the United States are used to thinking of our family histories in terms of decades or generations. We are astounded when we meet a member of the Daughters of the American Revolution who can trace her ancestry back three or four hundred years.

However, in societies that have had less migration and more social cohesion over time, family histories often can be traced back much further. We, the co-authors of this book, are Americans who fall into the latter category. Our Yun family clan, Papyeong Yun, is the largest of the Yun clans in Korea. Our ancestry traces back to General Shin-dal Yun, born in 892 CE,[4] who served Taejo Wang Geon in founding the Goryeo Dynasty, which ruled the Korean peninsula until the end of the 14th century.[5] The exonym "Korea" is derived from the name Goryeo.

We are 37th- and 38th-generation descendants, respectively, of General Shin-dal Yun. We have spent time in both our quaint ancestral hometown—a rice farming village that has never had a male resident with a surname other than Yun—and the differently quaint vortex of digital change that is Silicon Valley.

Joon Yun, who is Conrad's brother and Jeremy's father, used to say to his father Sung Hee Yun that the stories he heard as a child about the Yun family from a thousand years ago just didn't seem real. To a ten-year-old, even a summer feels long, so a thousand years seemed like an unbridgeable eternity. As he approached age fifty, however, Joon was stunned at how his five decades of life had gone by in a blink. A thousand years, he realized one day, adds up to just twenty of those blinks. Indeed, ten thousand years of recorded human history—the span consid-

---

4. CE denotes Common Era, a recent convention replacing AD (Anno Domini).
5. See https://en.wikipedia.org/wiki/Yoon_(Korean_surname); https://en.wikipedia.org/wiki/Goryeo.

ered in this book—is only two hundred blinks of an eye in terms of lived human experience.

From this perspective, we can feel a sense of proximity, even intimacy, with ancestors from a thousand or even ten thousand years ago. Relative to the arc of history, the people we call our ancestors can be seen as our contemporaries who lived in approximately the same brief epoch. We are them, and they are us.

If the people who lived during the last ten thousand years are our contemporaries, then who were our truly ancient ancestors? What do we know with confidence about their lives, their aspirations, and their fears? For the most part, not much, as we have almost no record of them.

On the other hand, we can surmise a few things. Before humans learned to harness communication, transportation, and energy technologies, they could travel only so far. Thus we can reasonably assume that prehistoric humans lived in social systems comprised of extended kin. To our knowledge, they had no means of communicating across distance.

On that single assumption alone, we can build an understanding of what life might have been like back in the prehistoric age.

Kin Skin in the Game

Social species exhibit a wide array of social behaviors that affect evolutionary fitness, including behaviors that relate to mating, foraging, survival, defense, communication, cooperation, and competition.

In this book, we are focused on social behaviors that are displayed when an individual has a vested interest in the success of another individual—for example, when they are closely related genetically. Evolution tends to select altruistic behaviors—sometimes even at the expense of one's own welfare—when they are associated with a net-positive outcome from the perspective of the kin group.[6]

---

6. Wilson, D. S., & Wilson, E. O. (2007). Rethinking the theoretical foundation of sociobiology. The Quarterly Review of Biology, 82, 327-348; https://doi.org/10.1086/522809.

This is called kin selection; the evolutionary fitness model associated with kin selection is known as inclusive fitness. The mathematical model behind kin selection is known as Hamilton's rule: the higher the degree of genetic relatedness, the higher the Darwinian payoff for altruistic behaviors.[7]

The phrase "skin in the game" is often used to refer to situations where we have something at stake in a social or business interaction—in short, we are personally invested in the outcome. Genetics can be a reason for having skin in the game. For example, we are more likely to be personally invested in the outcome of a Little League game one of our own children is playing in than one in which no relations are playing. The same is true of events in which even a distant cousin is competing: we simply are more likely to care than we would in the absence of this relationship. In this book we use our own version of "skin in the game" that reflects genetic proximity: "kin skin in the game."

The implications of not having kin skin in the game cannot be underestimated. As mentioned earlier, kin selection predicts the selection of otherwise inexplicable behaviors, such as those that are detrimental to oneself but beneficial to others in our kin group. To understand the power of kin skin in the game in driving evolutionary success, it is worth examining the social behaviors of non-human species that live together in communities exhibiting an exceptionally high degree of genetic relatedness.[8]

Eusociality

Eusociality is the highest level of organization of animal sociality.[9] It is defined by features such as cooperative brood care, overlapping generations living together, and a division into reproductive and non-reproductive groups.

7. See https://en.wikipedia.org/wiki/Kin_selection.
8. Hamilton, W. D. (1996). Narrow roads of gene land: The collected papers of W. D. Hamilton. Oxford, UK: W. H. Freeman/Spektrum.
9. See https://en.wikipedia.org/wiki/Eusociality.

The basis of their unusually high degree of cooperation is genetic alignment. Among eusocial insects such as termites and those belonging to the Hymenoptera order (ants, bees, and wasps), females often are more closely related (¾) to their sisters than to their daughters (½). Cooperation among sisters is unusually advantageous, and helping the queen give birth to more sisters propagates one's genes more than reproducing oneself.[10] Thus, in eusocial species, the queen and king often do all the reproducing while the sterile workers organize into a labor force that supports the overall hive.[11]

The degrees of cooperation and self-sacrifice among Hymenoptera are remarkable. For example, in Myrmecocystus mexicanus, sterile females fill their abdomens with liquid food and hang from the ceiling of the underground nest to provide food storage for the rest of the colony.[12] In Scaptotrigona postica, young workers provision the cell broods while older workers forage.[13] In some termite species, the soldiers have jaws so enlarged for defense and attack that they are unable to feed themselves and must be fed by workers.[14]

The benefits of such coordinated cooperation enabled by a high-degree of relatedness are evident in the sheer success of such species. Even though eusociality is thought to have emerged relatively recently (only around 150 million

10. In these species, an offspring's gender is typically determined by the number of chromosomes an individual possesses. Fertilized eggs have two sets of chromosomes (one from each parent) and develop into diploid females. Unfertilized eggs have only one set (from the mother) and develop into haploid males. This phenomenon is called haplodiploidy. Weinstock, G. M., Robinson, G. E., & the Honeybee Genome Sequencing Consortium. (2006). Insights into social insects from the genome of the honeybee apis mellifera. Nature, 443, 931-949; Cowan, D. P. & Stahlhut, J. K. (2004, July 13). Functionally reproductive diploid and haploid males in an inbreeding hymenopteran with complementary sex determination. PNAS, 101, 10374-0379.

11. Hölldobler, B. (1990). The ants. Cambridge, MA: Belknap Press.

12. Conway, J. R. (1986). The biology of honey ants. The American Biology Teacher, 48, 335-343.

13. van Veen, J. W., Sommeijer, M. J., & Meeuwsen F. (1997). Behaviour of drones in Melipona (Apidae, Meliponinae). Insectes Sociaux, 44, 435-447. doi:10.1007/s000400050063.

14. Adams, E. S. (1987). Territory size and population limits in mangrove termites. Journal of Animal Ecology, 56, 1069-1081.

years ago), eusocial insects account for a disproportionate percentage of the earth's biomass—up to half in some regions.[15] As E. O. Wilson observed, "Social insects are at the ecological center."[16]

The human kin tribe of prehistoric times can also be thought of as a hive of genetic relatives. According to Hamilton's rule, we took care of each other according to our degree of relatedness. We were largely supported by people who had our best interests at heart.

The departure from our prehistoric kin tribe roots is where the rest of this story begins.

---

15. Thorne, B. L., Grimaldi, D. A., & Krishna, K. (2001). Early fossil history of the termites. In Abe, T., Bignell, D. E., & Higashi, M. (Eds.). Termites: Evolution, sociality, symbioses, ecology (pp. 77-93). Springer; see also http://antbase.org/SISG/sibiodiversity.htm.
16. See http://antbase.org/SISG/sibiodiversity.htm.

CHAPTER TWO

Kin Diaspora and Social Entropy

Kin Diaspora

Over the generations, the degree of relatedness among branches of a family lineage declines. To promote outbreeding, evolution selects against incest by deterring attraction to close kin and through the existence of deleterious homozygous genetic diseases.[17] Social taboos against incest are also common.[18]

Put differently, a house naturally divides, and the divided houses keep dividing. The genetic alignment of the original house gets increasingly diluted with each generation, but each new kin hive is internally just as closely aligned genetically as was the original hive.[19] The lineages of Cain and Abel in the biblical narrative were never as genetically close as the brothers themselves. Kin altruism is reborn with every new hive, but competition between hives grows over the generations as genetic alignment disappears. Family branches inexorably become estranged over the generations.

We will see as we proceed that the division, dispersal, and genetic fragmentation of kin tribes are features of social evolution, not bugs. They promote diversity, intergroup competition, and memetic parallax—that is, the human tendency

---

17. See https://www.ncbi.nlm.nih.gov/pmc/articles/PMC3684741/; https://www.ncbi.nlm.nih.gov/pubmed/24179077.
18. Wilson, E. O. (2012). *The social conquest of earth*. New York: Liverwright, p. 199.
19. The resulting structure is fractal in nature, with each genealogical level replicating the proximity relationships that exist at the next higher order.

to see better when offered multiple vantage points (to be discussed later). They also help maintain a self-regulated balance between cooperative and competitive instincts in the lineage network. The central house might have stayed put while new branches migrated to new territories. This balance of ingroup attractive forces and outgroup repulsive forces, when viewed at scale, helped maintain the kin hive structure as mass human migration took hold during the prehistoric age.[20]

The human diaspora was under way.

Social Entropy and Rising Relationship Liquidity

Two things happened subsequently that warrant mention.

First, human dispersal began to reach geographic limits. As humans started to fill various geographic niches around the planet, collisions between tribes with little genetic alignment became more frequent and relative strangers were forced to contend with one another.

Second, humans acquired the so-called Promethean Fire[21]—the knowledge and tools that enabled them to shape their own future. When humans began harnessing energy, early on through horses and later through hydrocarbons, it enabled breathtaking progress, but it also increased the probability that competing tribes with little genetic alignment would collide with each other.

The increasing collision of tribes had profound effects, which to a significant extent were bloody. The diaspora that had started in humanity's cradle began to eat itself, and the slaughter of strangers and hegemony over the vanquished became all too common. On the other hand, trading of ideas and goods also began to flourish.

Energy increases the entropy of systems, and social entropy is no different. As human social systems harnessed energy, relationship liquidity—defined as the average number of people connected to a particular person and the potential number of transactions among them—vastly increased. There are many bene-

20. See https://en.wikipedia.org/wiki/Human_migration.
21. See https://en.wikipedia.org/wiki/Prometheus.

ficial aspects to a rising number of interpersonal interactions. Having access to more people can increase the probability of finding better partners, in life and in business.

Over time, as converging cultures blended into melting pots, unprecedented levels of prosperity ensued. To be sure, in addition to the propulsive forces of kin dispersal, a different force—the centripetal force of migration toward greener pastures of opportunity—also drew us away from each other and into agglomerative forces of human connection, such as cities. As Jane Jacobs chronicled in her work, The Economy of Cities, the diversity of people who gathered in the world's first cities came with a diversity of ideas. This dynamic set into motion a positive feedback of city inventiveness and city growth that propelled humanity from the Iron Age through the Space Age and to the present day.

Decreasing Genetic Alignment in Melting Pots

As the work of Jane Jacobs exemplifies, we have come to understand and appreciate the myriad benefits of humanity's global diaspora and the advent of diverse communities it catalyzed. Less appreciated is the cost of the shift from high alignment to low alignment (genetically speaking) that was an integral and unavoidable element of these changes. Our attraction to social novelty was shaped when our choices were far more limited than they are today. Not unlike our tendency to be drawn to sweet, fatty, and salty foods, there was little selection pressure in the Old World for the evolving upper limits of our attraction to new social opportunities. Social overload resulted in a higher quantity, but lower average quality, of human relationships. Furthermore, the ability to forsake existing relationships for new ones increased as the cost of doing so declined.

But an even deeper issue was emerging.

These melting pot communities exhibited an issue that would have been completely foreign to a kin tribe of the prehistoric age: the need to coexist within the context of low genetic alignment. Due to rising social entropy, the strong, stable bonds of small kin tribes had been replaced by weaker, transactional relationships among strangers who did not have kin skin in the game.

The twin fallouts from increased social entropy—declining genetic alignment and increased relationship liquidity—led to the following three phenomena: (1) increased self-dealing; (2) increased counterparty risk; (3) decreased win-win transactions that are based on vested interests.

Despite the huge capacity for prosperity enabled by the convergence of tribes, the potential for abuse was also increasing. Given the risks of abuse, trying to build a Great Society has been trying, to say the least.

Decline of Kin Skin in the Game Increases Self-Dealing

Let's delve further into what we mean by the term self-dealing.

Self-dealing isn't simply acting in one's own interest; everyone does that to a greater or lesser degree. Our individual tendency to act in our self-interest isn't a flaw of the evolutionary process but the core driver—in short, the urge to survive.

Self-dealing also isn't about criminality. A farmer who delivers spoiled produce or a contractor who pockets an advance payment and disappears before finishing the job are not self-dealing. They are just dishonest.

For the purposes of this book, the concept of self-dealing describes a behavior that is more complex than simple thievery and banditry, and that makes sense only in a world that has evolved past the truly primal "law of the jungle." Self-dealing exists only in the more advanced social world of bonds, oaths, covenants, and kinship. In other words, self-dealing only makes sense when the self-dealing parties have made commitments to act in the interest of others, even while likely still acting in their own interests.

The category of self-dealing that is easiest to define includes corruption and treachery: the explicit violation of an oath or vow of duty. This could be a city employee who takes a bribe when awarding a construction contract, thereby prioritizing personal gain over public duty. Or it could be a corporate CEO who invests the company's cash in a cousin-owned business on non-market terms. Such cases are all too common, as we all know.

A second type of self-dealing that is subtler is also more pervasive and corrosive. Consider an employee who participates in a frequent-flyer program. His obligation when traveling for work is to go with the lowest cost option, all other factors being equal. However, his actions are not necessarily aligned with his boss's or the company's best interests because he has an incentive to book a flight that will add to his frequent-flyer miles. This is an everyday example of self-dealing, in that the employee is enticed to put his own interests ahead of the interests to which he is socially bound—those of his boss and the company.

Some people might feel it's no big deal if an employee pays ninety dollars more for a flight in order to get enough frequent-flyer miles to book a free flight for his personal travel—people face similar small temptations all the time. The magnitude of the employee's self-dealing is not our concern in picking this example. Our point here is that such enticements to self-dealing are ubiquitous. They are embedded in our existence today, much as kin skin in the game has been the norm for most of human history.

However, in the era of rising relationship liquidity and low genetic alignment, self-dealing by those who have a duty to others has emerged as the most consequential maladaptation of human social evolution.

Kin skin in the game is nature's deterrent against the abuses of self-dealing. As kin skin in the game declines, the principal-agent risk rises. However, the human tendency to trust others was wired during the tribal era when kin skin in the game was higher. This misalignment of interests increases the incentives for exploitation, and those who violate trust have more opportunities to start new relationships than ever before, thereby reducing the cost of being detected.

Agency risk is proliferating in modern life. Corporate leaders are accused of enriching themselves at the expense of shareholders. Political leaders are accused of dealing for themselves at the expense of citizens. The problem is endemic everywhere that humans have a duty to others.

Decline of Kin Skin in the Game
Increases Counterparty Risk

In the preceding section, we discussed how the loss of kin skin in the game weakens the deterrence against self-dealing when a fiduciary obligation or some type of covenant exists. In the current section, we discuss how the loss of kin skin in the game and rising relationship liquidity weaken the protection against counterparty risk in situations where such obligations do not exist.

At its foundation, microeconomic theory is built on the assumption that voluntary exchanges that occur when perfect information is available are mutually beneficial. This is a very reasonable starting point: if I willingly trade my bicycle for your phone, then I must value the bicycle more than your phone, and the inverse is true for you. If not, why would we trade?

Usually this assumption is attacked on the basis of the underlying assumption of rationality. "People are not calculating automatons," the critique often goes. "People are motivated by all sorts of things other than gain."

In reality, this is a weak argument. Maybe your phone is broken and my bicycle is new, and I engage in the trade because you are my friend and I know you need a bicycle. In that case, the benefit I derive from the exchange is psychic—it has little to do with getting the phone—and the exchange is mutually beneficial. Whether you choose to call any trade "rational" or "irrational" is really just a matter of semantics.

The far bigger issue has to do with the assumption that information is being perfectly shared before the exchange.[22] You may be able to scrutinize and test-ride my bicycle before we trade, and I may be able to try out your phone. However, under almost any circumstance, you will know more about your phone than I do,

---

22. Think about the difference between a family dinner table, a neighborhood restaurant, and a lunch counter in a busy train station in, say, the 1970s—or any time before the age of franchises and reputation-tracking apps. On the one hand, the pattern of repeat encounters deterred the self-dealing that might have accompanied the attitude of "Who cares? You'll never see him again." On the other hand, within the kin tribe there is every reason to act with the interests of the other in mind. Kin tribesmen will see one another again, and as a consequence they do care.

and I will know more about my bicycle. This means that we each have the power to cheat each other by withholding relevant information.

Asymmetries of information introduce one significant vector by which voluntary transactions can be win-lose. Whichever party has the most information has the greatest latitude to cheat.

The behavior of cigarette manufacturers over the decades from the late 1950s to the early 2000s offers a case in point. Cigarette buyers during that era bought cigarettes willingly. However, they did so without the benefit of evidence the cigarette companies held regarding the severely adverse health consequences of smoking. Withholding this information turned a routine, win-win market transaction into a win-lose.

While the cigarette industry's campaign of active disinformation that denied the carcinogenic effects of smoking is well-known, it is hardly exceptional. Similar tactics are employed by Big Food, Big Data, and many more—not the least of which is Big Government.

The underlying reality in all these cases: what you don't know most definitely can hurt you.

The loss of kin skin in the game has weakened the natural deterrent against seeking win-lose transactions and increased counterparty risk. As a result, the prevalence of such zero-sum transactions has become all too common.

Decline of Kin Skin in the Game Decreases Win-Win Transactions Enabled by Vested Interests

There's an even more important driver of altruism within kin tribes than merely the deterrence against abuses. A kind act between relatives promotes inclusive fitness and motivates both the actor and the recipient to "expand the pie" as a way to drive win-win outcomes.

The loss of kin skin in the game doesn't only increase counterparty risk and the potential for downside, win-lose transactions; it also blunts any distinct vested incentives for seeking win-win transactions.

While trades among counterparties enable all sorts of win-win transactions (such as the example of trading a bicycle for a phone between strangers discussed in the prior section), the vested interest of kin skin in the game is a powerful and entirely different type of win-win: it allows a person to win from an inclusive fitness perspective by virtue of another person winning. For example, an aunt who spends time educating a nephew about how to distinguish between poisonous and edible mushrooms is improving the evolutionary fitness both of her nephew and herself.

In that sense, kin skin in the game incentivizes cooperative behaviors.[23] Whether in a beehive or a human kin tribe, altruistic behaviors that enabled win-wins were likely far more prevalent in a genetically aligned community than in today's community of strangers.

Decline of Kin Skin in the Game among Neighbors and Communities

There is one social institution, however, that hasn't been rendered transactional by the effects of rising social entropy: the nuclear family.

Communities now are largely siloes of nuclear families living among other families with whom they share low genetic alignment. Physical walls go up between properties, and emotional walls go up between neighbors. Within each nuclear family, self-dealing is disfavored, win-lose transactions are disfavored, and win-win transactions based on vested interests are favored. Between adjacent nuclear families that have no mutual kin skin in the game, each of these trends begins to reverse itself to some degree: deterrence against self-dealing is weaker, deterrence against win-lose transactions is weaker, and win-win transactions based on vested interests are less favored.

---

23. To some extent, hints of this type of thinking is already out there. Many successful organizations, companies, and sports teams call themselves a family. The family framing is an aspiration for the ethos of kin tribes by modern, non-kin groups. Some organizations pay bonuses for team or company success rather than individual performance.

If anything, as genetic relatedness between neighboring families has fallen, the kin altruism within each family has become a stronger phenomenon. Since fewer extended kin live near enough to draw altruistic efforts from the nuclear family, people end up concentrating nearly all of their kin altruistic energy on their own nuclear family. This helps explain the explosion of helicopter parenting and over-investment in children commonly observed today.

In America today, the nuclear family is archetypal: two parents, 2.2 children (and falling), and possibly one pet. One observation about modern families is that many parents seem to martyr themselves to their children, giving up careers, marital accord, sleep, exercise, social life, etc. They are so focused on their kids that they might miss a social gathering rather than miss their son's baseball game. Related to this is the broad observation that people seem to be under-invested in their neighborhoods.

These twin observations—people over-investing in their kids and under-investing in their neighbors—are part and parcel of the same underlying phenomenon: a subconscious acting out of Hamilton's rule of altruism based on the degree of relatedness. Few would admit they are doing this and even fewer are aware that they are agents of deeper genetic programming. Nevertheless, it is a reality, and many feel it isn't quite right to live this way. The reason is that our social sensibilities are wired for a time when we lived in kin tribes, like the Yun clan.

Let's take a closer look at the modern family through the lens of kin skin in the game. In general, moms do not use their children for their own benefit; they take action and make decisions in ways that help their children. When it comes to their children, moms typically do not self-deal.

What is true of moms is also true of dads and, to a lesser degree, of siblings, aunts, uncles, and cousins. Most of us do not use the fact that we are related to put our own interests above our shared bonds—in short, our blood relatives are less likely to self-deal in their interactions with us than (kin) strangers. As the saying goes, "Blood is thicker than water."

Put more accurately, altruism towards kin is a form of self-dealing, as serving kin benefits the server. The difference between this type of self-dealing and those mentioned previously could not be more profound. In the former case, one wins by virtue of another person winning. In the latter case, one wins at the expense of another person.

The Rise of Institutions

As we know, wonderful things have happened to the human species over the past ten thousand years or so. Our numbers have grown exponentially. We live over twice as long as our near-ancestors did even two hundred years ago. We occupy as many evolutionary niches on the planet as almost any other mammal.

However, not every dimension of the human experience has improved over the past ten millennia. Over the span of those two hundred "blinks" of a human life, we lost the foundation of our social architecture: kin tribes.

Among more and more societies throughout the world today, the nuclear family has taken the role of the kin tribe as the integral social institution reflecting inclusive fitness. Beyond that, we largely live in communities of genetic strangers. We are now highly interconnected and belong not to one group but to overlapping networks based on our family, gender, ethnic group, language, neighborhood, company, college alumni, eye color, favorite sports team, etc.

This shift from high-alignment to low-alignment social systems has fundamentally changed the social calculus. Based on inclusive fitness, strangers have an incentive to self-deal and to put their own interests ahead of others'.

However, the biologic evolution of our social brain can't keep pace with cultural evolution and so we underestimate the counterparty risk posed by strangers. Thus, we have long been trying to build institutions to help us adapt. Many types of social, political, and economic institutions have been created. For example, dating back at least to the Code of Hammurabi, legal institutions have been created to orient human behavior around incentives and disincentives.

To some extent these institutions have served us well, but they have failed to create a system of vested interest in others to replace inclusive fitness as the essential social contract. As we will see in the next chapter, the beginnings of these institutions largely coincide with the recorded history of human civilizations.

CHAPTER THREE

A Brief (Institutional) History of the World

Somewhere along the long journey to the advent of the first cities in Anatolia and Mesopotamia roughly ten thousand years ago, the stewardship that held tribes together was supplanted by the leadership of kings and emperors. Whereas stewardship implies actions taken by a few in the service of the many, the definition of leadership has no such limitations. Indeed, without having kin skin in the game, this new category of human social actor, the "leader," was less incentivized to put the interests of the people before his or her own interests.[24]

All empires and monarchies—from Akkad, Assyria, and Babylon to those of modern times—have been undermined by a lack of incentive structures to replace

---

24. Look at the promotional materials for business schools anywhere and you'll be hard pressed to find a page, or even a paragraph, that doesn't include the word "leadership." In fact, the biggest business idea of our time isn't leadership. It's one that is all but absent from the business school curricula and the public discussion: stewardship. Stewardship is defined as having the responsibility to shepherd and safeguard the interests of others. Many people are in formally defined positions of stewardship in public corporations, private enterprises, and charitable organizations. Warren Buffett, one of the most widely admired business leaders of our time, is among the few public figures who speaks regularly of the importance of stewardship in business. It is striking, then, to see the dearth of courses addressing the concept of stewardship at top U.S. business schools. As of 2014, in the online course catalogs of the top five MBA programs in the United States (as ranked by U.S. News & World Report), "stewardship" is nowhere to be found in any course title. To put this into context, each of these schools offers at least five classes with the word "leadership" in the title. Fortunately, stewardship is an innate trait. It is observed throughout nature and is exemplified by the nurturing instincts among kin. These behaviors were evolutionarily selected to meet the needs of kin-based social systems. For humans it did so during the prehistoric age that shaped human selection. In the Darwinian calculus, altruistic behavior toward kin can enhance one's own evolutionary fitness—the phenomenon of inclusive fitness. Put another way, it is our nature to nurture. While such behaviors were likely selected and proved beneficial when humans lived in kin-based tribes, in our current world of easy mobility and accelerating social dispersal, communities typically develop around diverse, non-kin populations. Many of our biologically wired factory-setting behaviors, including the degree to which we trust our fiduciaries and agents, are rendered maladaptive in a world of high-liquidity relationships that are largely transaction oriented.

the inclusive fitness that characterized kin tribes. Corruption, oppression, and self-dealing were the rule, not the exception. Tyranny could be maintained over the generations through the codification of nepotism, which exemplified the perils of inclusive fitness narrowly applied at the expense of collective interests. For quite a while, history was a story of sovereigns ruling over the people instead of on behalf of the people.

Eventually, some societies envisioned governance models in which a chosen few would rule on behalf of the people. Republics emerged in multiple parts of the world, including ancient Europe, the ancient Near East, and Africa.[25] Although a lot of thought went into nurturing these republics, they lacked a critical feature. None of them developed a system of vested interest in the people commensurate to the inclusive fitness of kin tribes.

Abuses not dissimilar to the types observed in totalitarian empires were inevitable. For example, the Roman Republic, which was formed after the Roman Kingdom was overthrown in 509 BCE, itself decayed into a travesty of governance until finally collapsing in 27 BCE with the establishment of the Roman Empire.

By the time Augustus appointed himself the first emperor of Rome—roughly seven centuries after the city was founded—the ubiquity of self-dealing created an opportunity for cultural arbitrage of epic proportions.

Into that world, in approximately the year 4 BCE, a certain future carpenter from Nazareth was born in Bethlehem. By the time that baby was a young man, he had taken to employing parables to remind people to use their power to act on behalf their dependents. One biblical story recounts how the Nazarene knelt to wash the feet of his disciples in a show of stewardship.[26]

After centuries of nepotistic leaders who gave the world to their sons, a story of a God who gave his only son to the world offered a powerful antithesis.

We know something else: that story caught on.

What made the story stand out was as much what it was not as what it was.

---

25. See https://en.wikipedia.org/wiki/Republic.
26. John 13:1-17.

What it was not was a continuation of thousands of years of accelerating human drift, away from stewardship within kin tribes (where we started) and toward the self-dealing and corruption of monarchs and emperors.

Over time, the magnitude of this story began to sink in. Eventually—a few centuries later—the story prompted one of the most unique events in the evolution of human civilizations: the resetting of the calendar. Whereas time had long been related to the reign of an emperor, the birth of Christ marked an effective "year zero" from which to measure all time.[27]

The resetting of the calendar that took place more than one thousand years ago persists to this day.

Why did resetting the calendar catch on when it did? As with most gradual change in culture or custom, there's no way to know for sure. However, it's clear that during the 9th and 10th centuries CE[28]—the depths of the so-called Dark Ages—the transformative promise offered in the story of Christ had devolved into a dystopia of disappointment. Just as the Greek and Roman republics had collapsed under the weight of corruption and self-dealing, so had the Catholic Church gradually done the same.[29]

One example of self-dealing by the Church was usury. The world of the early Middle Ages was characterized by deflation and zero economic growth. Lending practices were frequently predatory, and more often than not the predators were priests. Perhaps surprisingly, the poor were not the only victims; nobles also forfeited property—even entire estates—to rapacious clerical moneylenders. The Church was powerful, but ultimately it responded to pressure to curb abusive practices within its ranks. By the start of the second millennium of the Common

27. Technically, the year 1 BCE was chosen to correspond with Christ's birth; later research found that the calibration was off, a better estimate being that Christ was born in roughly 4 BCE.
28. See https://en.wikipedia.org/wiki/Common_Era.
29. Governors of the Roman Empire initially persecuted members of this rising institution. In the year 380 CE, however, Christianity became the State Church of the Roman Empire, halting centuries of official religious persecution.

Era, the Church's collapse into self-dealing was so complete that the Pope himself had to intervene. In 1049, Pope Leo IX outlawed interest-bearing loans, declaring at the Council of Reims that "no cleric or layman should be a usurer."

Persecution of Christians by the Roman Emperor had given way to exploitation of Christians by the Church. Along the way, feudalism had been born.

A funny thing happened when Pope Leo IX outlawed usury: trade in interest-bearing loans—now officially outlawed by the Church—took off. With the usurious inclinations of the clergy at least partially restrained, the medieval version of the private financial sector stepped in and opened up a new market space. At the center of this space was a financial innovation known as the bill of exchange, the predecessor to today's bank check. Bills of exchange were important not only because they made it possible for commerce to take place over long distances, which facilitated trade, but also—and importantly—because they constituted a loophole in the papal ban on interest-bearing loans. By carefully designing their terms, the earliest merchant bankers could employ bills of exchange as a way to extend short-term loans. So arose in the history of humanity a new species: the financial services professional.

Within a couple of centuries, the transformative financial service innovation that was the invention of bills of exchange was complemented by an equally transformative legal innovation: the joint-stock company.

The corporation had been born.[30]

The combination of innovations in financial services with those in what we today refer to as corporate governance had far-reaching and dramatic effects. The very word "corporation"— its root being the Latin corpus or body—tells the

---

30. In contemporary corporate law, reference to a joint-stock company is most often considered synonymous with a combination of incorporation (a legal identity that is distinct from that of the shareholders) and limited liability (shareholders are liable for company debts only to the extent of the funds they invested). This is why joint-stock companies are often known as corporations or limited companies.

story. Legal innovation literally created new "bodies" that had their own rights and responsibilities, distinct from human bodies.

However, these paired innovations also created what economists refer to as a principal-agent problem. In this case, the role of the principal is held by the stockholders, while the role of the agent is held by the firm's managers and board of directors (who in theory have a fiduciary duty to shareholders but may be tempted to serve their own interests).[31] In a human body, the brain and the muscles are aligned, and both have an interest in the survival of the individual corpus. In the case of a corporation, the brains (the shareholders) may or may not align with the muscles (the company's management and directors). When this alignment doesn't exist, corporate failure is inevitable.

Thus, not long after its invention, the corporation became the newest institutional vessel for abuse of the people. By the 19th century, the emergence of the factory and large-scale corporate production created a division that defined much of the economics and politics of the 20th century: the division between capital and labor. The problem was famously framed by Karl Marx, who spoke of the exploitation of a proletarian worker class by the owners of capital, who extracted the lion's share of the value produced and left a bare minimum to the workers. Absent a revolution, the dominant solution to this problem from the workers' standpoint, which emerged in the 19th century, was to organize labor in order to bargain more effectively for an equitable share of the production returns. This new corpus, which sat across the bargaining table from the corporation, was the trade union.

Meanwhile, political parties throughout the industrialized world were adapting to the new realities: one party, usually framed as the conservatives, championed the interests of capital, while an opposing party, usually framed as progressives or socialists, championed the interests of labor. From that point on until the present day, relations between labor and capital—which is to say, between trade unions

---

31.   The joint-stock company was an innovation that eventually enabled owners to give stock to managers as a way to foster congruent goals.

and corporate interests—were (at best) zero-sum battles that often deteriorated into negative-sum tactics, violence, or all-out war.

At least one 19th-century economist, William Jevons, had a different idea of how to manage the newly emergent tension between capital and labor. Jevons was one of the three primary architects of the mathematical substructure of modern economics, which is referred to as neoclassical economics to distinguish it from the classical economics of Adam Smith and David Ricardo.

Unlike many of his contemporary economists, Liverpool-born Jevons had witnessed the misery of the factory classes firsthand and was highly sensitive to their plight. "Does not everyone feel that there is an evil at work which needs remedy?" Jevons wrote. "Does not the constant occurrence of strikes, and the rise of vast and powerful organisations of workmen, show that there is some profound unfitness in the present customs of the country to the progress of affairs?" Arguing for the imperative of institutional innovation as eloquently as any modern advocate of equity, Jevons stated, "If the masters insist on retaining their ancient customs; if they will shroud their profits in mystery, and treat their men as if they were another class of beings, whose interests are wholly separate and opposite; I see trouble in the future as in the past."

Jevons continued, "I hope to see the time when workmen will be to a great extent their own capitalists ... I believe that a movement of workmen towards co-operation in the raising of capital would be anticipated by employers admitting their men to a considerable share of their profits."[32]

A century later, the approach for which Jevons advocated became the new normal. New companies across the United States began to adopt a corporate innovation particularly well-suited to the emerging information age: employee stock options. Issuing stock options promised to accomplish the goal Jevons articulated—the alignment of labor and capital—at the same time it resolved the

32. Auerswald, P. (2017). *The code economy: A forty-thousand-year history.* New York: Oxford University Press, pp. 92-93.

principal-agent problem inherent in the corporate structure. Because a corporation's workers were also its owners, capital and labor would work together. The corporate mind and muscles were aligned.

The effective use of stock options for all employees is one significant element of the mix that made Silicon Valley the entrepreneurial juggernaut it has become and, as a consequence, has helped to fuel the information age.

At the turn of the millennium, it seemed to many people working in technology that we were on the cusp of a special new era of human history. Alongside institutional innovations like stock options, the invention and growth of the Internet held out the promise of a boundless and inclusive future. The brutal conflict between capital and labor that had defined the ideological battles of the 20th century would give way to a collaborative era in which ownership itself would gradually evaporate in the sunshine of digital equity. Humanity's accumulated knowledge was suddenly available to almost anyone, anywhere. Open-source projects were creating a new paradigm for the world of work—horizontal and distributed rather than hierarchical and centralized. Location would matter less, while talent would matter more.

The endless cycle of institutional Whack-a-Mole seemed to have come to an end at last. On a free and open Internet driven by mission-aligned teams of creators, the degeneration into self-dealing that had characterized one historical wave after another for two millennia had come to an end at last. Or so we thought.

Little did the Internet idealists foresee a coming era when these companies would be exposed as self-expanding corporate monsters who, as has been the case with every type of institution since the end of the tribal era, grow by self-dealing at the expense of the people.

Silicon Valley companies are now being exposed as the latest institutions that don't serve the public's interests as well as they serve their own. Clickbaiting to maximize profits and misusing consumer data reflect a company-over-customer philosophy.

Looking back, empires, republics, religious institutions, and corporations exhibited a grow-or-die tendency. Think of conquests, crusades, colonialism, and imperialism as phenomena that "fed the beast." When these institutions did die, sometimes through violent revolutions, their replacements failed to address the central issue—the need to develop commensurate incentive structures to replace inclusive fitness. Pete Townshend anthemized this Sisyphean hell of revolutions: "Meet the new boss. Same as the old boss."

The highs have been higher but the lows have often been lower. We've reacted, but none of the solutions we've offered quite worked out over time, even if they seemed sound initially. And we've never quite figured out why.

These examples demonstrate a recurring theme: unless first-order alignment issues are addressed, solutions to second-order problems will only create derivative ones. World history as we know it has largely been an epiphenomenon of the central story of mismanaging our transition from the inclusive fitness of the tribal era to modern times.

Fifty years ago, the ills of the world tended to be framed in terms of the movements that we undertook to address them. We remember the racism of the era in the frame of the civil rights movement. We remember the sexism of the era in the frame of the women's liberation movement. We remember Vietnam and the massacre at Kent State in the frame of the anti-war movement.

Today we frame the ills of the world as epidemics. The opioid epidemic. The obesity epidemic. The polarization epidemic. It is as if we have lost our capacity to act to create the world we live in and are reduced to functioning as passive vectors of transmission for one or another social virus.

This could not be farther from reality. Pulling back the curtain just a bit on the various boogeymen we presume to be the cause of these epidemics, we ultimately find that—just as in a biological epidemic—each of us is both the cause and the victim of the ills we face.

Fifty years ago we dedicated ourselves to putting a man on the moon. Today we stand firmly on earth, shoulders slightly hunched, eyes fixed on our screens, watching the minute-by-minute unfolding of the unifying spectacle of our age, our one genuine movement: the race to the bottom line.

PART II

Race to the Bottom (Line)

CHAPTER FOUR

The Change that Mattered Most

Picture this. In the historical drama film Gladiator, which depicted the Roman Empire as it was heading toward collapse, Maximus, the blood sport's rising star who was challenging the corruption of a philistine society, does a product endorsement.

Between death matches.

For olive oil.

If you think that sounds too absurd, even for a movie about a circus-like era of human history, so did the movie's producers. They deleted this scene from the script because they thought the idea of a gladiator doing commercial endorsements detracted from the realistic feel of the story.[33]

Yet the reality is that gladiators in Ancient Rome did in fact use their celebrity to endorse products.[34] The frescos and graffiti of the gladiator era suggest that people back then trusted the purchase advice of their superstar heroes just as they do today.

There is a powerful scene in the movie when young Lucius approaches Maximus as the latter is about to enter the arena.[35] The poignant moment portrays the influence celebrity athletes wield over children who idolize them. The scene is not dissimilar to that depicted in one of the most successful product endorsements

33. See https://www.ign.com/articles/2000/02/10/not-such-a-wonderful-life-a-look-at-history-in-gladiator.

34. See http://faculty.uml.edu/ethan_spanier/teaching/documents/cyrinogladiator.pdf.

35. See https://getyarn.io/yarn-clip/20e01580-7afe-4eb5-8fef-5f6e61e65ba0.

of all-time: Coke's campaign in which a wounded Mean Joe Greene is offered a Coke in the tunnel of an arena by a wide-eyed young fanboy, who is thanked with a smile.[36]

In the prehistoric kin tribe era, our larger-than-life role models would have been our aunts and uncles or even our parents. This familial sense is evoked in the Lucius-Maximus scene in Gladiator, as Lucius is fatherless and Maximus's own son has been murdered. From an inclusive fitness perspective, idolizing and modeling our lives after the celebrities in our prehistoric kin tribe and trusting the ideas and products they endorsed would have served us well. In other words, evolution selected for an innate tendency to trust the endorsements of our avuncular (uncle) and materteral (aunt) heroes.

Two of the authors of this book are a nephew-uncle pair. We live within five minutes of each other. The avuncular and materteral influences of our tribal past have disappeared from our daily lives and been replaced by strangers who don't have kin skin in the game. Modern day celebrities and so-called heroes have an incentive to self-deal and exploit their worshipers for personal gain through extractive capitalism.

Just as Coke made a lot of money at the expense of children who reflexively and almost unavoidably followed their genetic scripting, trusting the ideas and products modern celebrities endorse is an evolutionary maladaptation.

The Evil Stepmother Effect

When it comes to what we receive from others, the change that has mattered most is who gives it to us.

Take food, for example. Until the modern age, our food was produced and prepared for us by someone who had our best interests at heart: our mothers. Our moms would never dream of adding something to our food to make us eat more or to save on the cost if there were serious doubts about the effect on our well-being.

---

36.   See https://www.youtube.com/watch?v=xffOCZYX6F8.

In the modern world, however, food largely comes from people who care about themselves first and about us second: the food industry. Being a secondary priority is a dangerous position to be in. And yet, there we are.

The food industry, which now baits the public through food to serve its own economic interests, is incentivized to do things to our food to make us eat more or to save on the cost despite doubts about the effects on our well-being. Our food system has shifted from being a high-alignment system during the kin tribe era to a low-alignment system today.

A million years ago, on the African savannah that is humanity's home, sweets were rare. Our earliest ancestors didn't buy tubs of gummy bears at Costco. They didn't buy orange juice by the half-gallon or consume boxes of breakfast cereal infused with corn syrup. They did, however, need food energy—and lots of it—to satisfy their caloric demands. As a consequence, humans evolved taste receptors a.k.a. our "sweet tooth," which helped guide us to fruits and other foods rich in nutritionally essential sugars. (We humans are not alone. Think of Winnie the Pooh's love of honey, a fiction based on biological reality: bears crave sugar too.)

Fast-forward to the past century, when the vast majority of people in industrialized countries and elsewhere sourced foods not through their own hunting and gathering but from a global agro-industrial complex. Processed foods—not just bags of potato chips and cans of soda but also baby formula and energy bars—are engineered to appeal to our ancient cravings for sugar, fat, and salt. Even fresh produce is the outcome of market-driven optimization, with fruit and vegetable varieties bred for appearance, transportability, and, of course, taste. To the delight of our Stone Age taste buds, sugar, fat, and salt sources today are cheap and abundant.[37]

That's just the beginning of the story. The standard process of market competition selects a few winners that work to preserve their market advantage, or industry associations are created to represent large groups of market incumbents—or

---

37. See https://www.nytimes.com/2012/06/06/opinion/evolutions-sweet-tooth.html; https://news.nationalgeographic.com/news/2015/01/150118-evolution-flavor-taste-hamburger-ngfood/.

both.[38] In the case of sugar and corn syrup, this process of industry consolidation has been helped along considerably by a U.S. government policy of protecting industry from market disruptions, which is encoded in a paragon of special interest legislation innocuously known as the Farm Bill. This policy, which stems from the deflationary trauma of the Great Depression, has, over the span of decades, led to the creation of government-sponsored agriculture industry cartels.[39]

What have been the consequences of this political self-dealing and evolutionary impulses run amok? Anyone with even one eye on public health issues in the United States and other industrialized countries in which similar dynamics have played out knows the answer: a deeply disturbing and far-reaching obesity epidemic that is a textbook case of how self-dealing actors can hijack evolutionary inclinations to their own advantage, using institutions (in this case, those of science and representational politics) as their tool.[40] Consumers seem all but resigned to the reality that the food industry will bait them with fake foods—and fake news about those fake foods.

Now, we are essentially consuming counterparty risk.

Seen from a higher perch, this dynamic is nefarious. Once upon a time, our mother—or other kin with a vested in interest in our success—gave us food. Now our food is largely produced by the one who has taken the position that once belonged to our moms but who does not have a vested interest in our success—the ever-present self-dealing archetype in Cinderella, Snow White, and other folklore tales: the evil stepmother.[41]

The Winner's Curse and the Commodification of Life

Why doesn't the bad behavior of the food industry get selected out? Can't we call out bad behaviors, regulate them, shame them, and make them go away?

38. See https://promarket.org/sugar-industry-buys-academia-politicians/; https://www.heritage.org/agriculture/report/sugar-shakedown-how-politicians-conspire-the-sugar-lobby-defraud-americas.
39. See https://www.heritage.org/agriculture/report/sugar-shakedown-how-politicians-conspire-the-sugar-lobby-defraud-americas.
40. See https://www.ncbi.nlm.nih.gov/pmc/articles/PMC3228640/.
41. See https://en.wikipedia.org/wiki/Stepmother.

Maybe.

In an ideal world, we would want a system that selects for the production (of products, information, and services) of maximum inherent value at the lowest cost. If the inherent value is rewarded by maximum external trading value earned, the system feeds itself in a self-reinforcing fashion.

Kin skin in the game incentivizes production for its inherent value. If a kin member benefits from receiving the product, information, or service, the producer succeeds as a function of the success of the receiver through inclusive fitness. Kin altruism plus free market competition is a race to the top.

In a low-alignment world that is based on trade among counterparties instead of on a vested interest in others, reciprocal altruism may step in where kin altruism weakens. Reciprocal altruism can produce win-wins through mutually beneficial transactions. High relationship liquidity, however, compromises that loyalty.[42]

Another way of understanding this phenomenon is through a concept in behavioral economics known as "The Winner's Curse," which refers to the tendency for the winning bid in an auction to exceed an item's true worth or intrinsic value. The winner's curse occurs because each participant in the auction has only partial information about the item, so some systematically overestimate its worth and others systematically underestimate it. Naturally those who overestimate it are more likely to bid high and thus "win" the auction.

Our version of The Winner's Curse comes with a twist. In the world of misaligned incentives and self-dealing, a variety of institutions will compete in the marketplace—think, for example, of investment banks in the years prior to the global financial crisis. Some investment banks might have been highly ethical and have refrained from adopting financial innovations such as the packaging and repacking of subprime mortgages as shaky collateralized debt obligations. Others

---

42. Without kin altruism and reciprocal altruism to protect the mutual benefits of a transaction, extractive transactions can emerge. Such exploitative transactions can occur through coercion, but they can also occur among mutually consenting parties, due to factors such as information asymmetry. In fact, in a corrupted system, the system may even be incentivized to select for greater degrees of information asymmetry over time to maximize the extraction.

embraced such practices eagerly, without regard for ethics or the aggregate consequences. With bond-rating agencies also involved in self-dealing and shirking their responsibility to downgrade suspect products, the worst performers from an ethical standpoint became the best performers from a market standpoint. It didn't take long, of course, for the worst practices to become the norm. Just as "bad money drives out good" according to Gresham's Law, so bad institutions drove out good ones in the race to the bottom line. We all know what happened next.

The counterparty risk of bad behavior could be mitigated if social entropy and relationship liquidity remain low. However, if social entropy, connectivity, and relationship liquidity are high, kin altruism and reciprocal altruism both fall and counterparty risk rises. This is where we are today: a world in which people largely produce products, information, and services that prioritize their external value—their trading or sales value—over their inherent value.

That shift in priority from inherent value to external value—an inevitable shift when the structure of society changes from high alignment to low alignment—changes everything. As we fall in rank from #1 in our mom's life to #2 in a stranger's life in so many of our life domains, it promotes a phenomenon called commodification.

Commodification is the creation of things for their trading value. One could make the case that producers are incentivized to maximize trading value. With proper feedback loops, symmetrical information, rational behavior, etc., the maximization of external value can also promote the maximization of inherent value. Reciprocal altruism is based on this. To some extent, the desire to produce products and services for trade is a motivator for the kind of innovation and cost reduction we've seen during the history of commerce.

This theoretical scenario, however, is often undermined. With low alignment and high relationship liquidity, it's darn near impossible to keep extractive capitalism in check. The negative feedback loop that would keep violators in check is not strong enough to deter exploitative behaviors.

Now add in unrestrained competition and it's a race to the bottom line. In a market of producers vying to sell, they maximize for trading value. Whereas we might hope that the maximization of trading value is associated with maximum inherent value, delivering inherent value is generally at least somewhat more costly. Competition, if anything, selects for lowest costs, which—in expected value terms at least—will be associated with lower inherent value. We therefore have a setup where the system selects for maximum commodification at the lowest cost, which is associated with the lowest inherent value.

Such is the race to the bottom line that we are in right now.

Today, the behavior of commodification is evident everywhere. It's not just institutions against the people. It's also people against the institutions. Students face increasing pressure to learn not for the inherent value of learning but with a focus on the external value (commodification) of that effort in competing for college admission.[43]

It's also people against each other. People too often engage in activities not for the inherent purpose but for the promotional purpose of signaling to others. Virtue was once pursued for its own sake; by contrast, virtue signaling is the commodification of virtue.[44] Cars were once bought for transportation; now, the signaling value of automobiles often exceeds the mechanical value. Clothes used to clothe a person; now fashion is about signaling. People used to live life for itself; they now too often attend events or travel for the purpose of promoting their personal brand on social media. None of us needs to work hard to come up with examples; in 21st-century life, these phenomena are anything but subtle.

Commodification has replaced the authentic original purpose everywhere there are relationships between strangers. Accounting used to serve the purpose of creating insights into one's family-owned business. Now accounting is often

---

43. Some might make the argument that the commodification of learning is a good thing, in that a certain portion of the population would not have studied as hard as they did had that effort not been made for the sake of gaining college admissions.
44. See https://en.wikipedia.org/wiki/Virtue_signalling.

misused to tell some fictional truths to sell stock to a stranger.[45] Language might once have been used predominantly to convey truth, but now it is far more often used to sell a story.

In the end, everyone is another's mark in this carnival.

And in the end, bad behavior drives out good behavior until only bad behavior is left. The system self-selects for extractive and exploitative institutions. If we force one media company to use less clickbait, another will use more in order to pick up the other's market share. If we force one food company to use less sugar, another will use more to fill the void in the market. In a way, the Kardashians and high-fructose corn syrup are really the same phenomenon—the inevitable outcome of a race to the bottom line, when misalignment meets unbridled capitalism.

No matter how many times we rerun this simulation called society, the system will eventually select for fake news about fake heroes endorsing fake foods.[46]

In the next chapter, we will examine several industries in the context of this race to the bottom line.

45. Barach L., & Gu, F. (2016). *The end of accounting and the path forward for investors and managers*. Hoboken, NJ: John Wiley & Sons.
46. See https://www.forbes.com/sites/brucelee/2016/10/03/spotting-fake-celebrity-endorsements-of-diet-and-health-remedies/#1a8f7696fdb2.

CHAPTER FIVE

Race to the Bottom Line

The change that has mattered most is the reality that people who act with our best interest at heart have been increasingly replaced with people who act with their own best interest at heart.

This change promotes the evolution of institutions toward prioritizing commodification, extraction, and exploitation over inherent value to the people.

The media, entertainment, sports, banking, and real estate industries offer a few examples.

Media

As was the case with food, when it comes to the information we receive from others, the change that has mattered most is who gives it to us.

We humans have an innate evolutionary tendency to trust information provided by others. Think about it. When our tribal leaders or brethren shared information back in the age of kin altruism, people could trust one thing: they did so with their kin's best interests at heart. Sure those leaders and brethren did not know much by today's terms, but when they did offer information—"There is a lion behind that tree" or "Don't drink that water"—it was in the service of their tribe's shared genetic interest. In such an environment, the human community evolved a culture of storytelling to convey information useful for survival.

Today, communications technologies and social media enable genetic strangers to control most of our information flow. Since they don't have kin skin in the game, their self-interest is to use information to exploit their audiences to maximize their own fitness. Unlike your mom, who put you first, the media industry cares first about itself and only secondarily about you, the customer. Moreover, the media industry today can dupe our moms and use them to indirectly exploit their own children—think of virtually every ad campaign targeting parents.

The purpose of information nowadays is for the trading value. By virtue of that commodification, the entire value system of the information economy has been corrupted. Media agents value velocity over veracity, often presenting the information most likely to maximize their evolutionary fitness using information as a weapon of mass distortion. The vast majority of information is actually noise masquerading as information intended to dupe the public in the service of extractive capitalism.

Even when the news is not fake, editors can fake its relevance in order to hijack our attention. For example, it may be true that a bear attack occurred halfway around the world, but including that story in our newsfeed distorts its relevance. With very few exceptions, the media today draws our attention to a seemingly endless parade of remote threats that are not in our immediate vicinity and therefore are mostly irrelevant to our evolutionary fitness.

Like our food, the interactions encouraged by digital media are designed to be heavy on stimulation and low on nourishment. Processed information is as harmful to the mind as processed food is to the body. The result is an epidemic of digitally enabled social gluttony that is every bit as debilitating as the obesity epidemic.

Entertainment

In her iconic photograph "American Girl in Italy" taken in 1951, Ruth Orkin portrays men ogling Ninalee Craig as she walked down a street in Florence. Despite the cultural stigma attached to the practice today, from an evolutionary perspective, prehistoric males who did not instinctively respond to visual cues about potential mates would face adverse evolutionary selection. In a similar fashion, when we drive past a car accident, we instinctively turn our heads to look. In nature, an organism that does not rubberneck at signs of carnage is ignoring useful cues about a threat in their vicinity, which could lead to adverse selection.

Traits shaped and culled during prior eras of evolution can be rendered maladaptive through contextual dislocation. Today, the entertainment industry lures viewers with manufactured scenes involving sex and violence. Without kin skin in the game, the industry is incentivized to exploit our hardwired tendency to rubberneck at such cues.

Our evolutionarily selected preference for social novelty is also being exploited by the social media industry. From an evolutionary standpoint, the attraction of social novelties makes sense. There are, after all, many beneficial aspects to an increasing number of possible social transactions, whether in romantic life, friendship, or business, as access to more people can increase the probability of finding good partners. But, in a world where access to social novelty is virtually limitless, does a tendency to be intrigued by new social opportunities on social media make us better off?

Our innate tendency to pay attention to status—our position within the social pecking order —is also being exploited by the entertainment industry. Status can affect access to resources, mating opportunities, and many other elements of evolutionary success.[47] The entertainment industry panders to our attraction to status by paying out for high-status performers and using camera angles and staging to make performers appear taller.[48]

A particular segment of the entertainment industry founded on our hardwired instinct to rubberneck at status deserves particular mention: sports.

Sports

For a significant part of the 20th century, Major League Baseball captivated the nation's imagination. Local teams were the pride, and in some ways the identity,

---

47. The luxury and glamour markets figured this out long ago. People seek constant reassurance of their status, and the consumer industry is ready to provide gaudier and gaudier symbols of status that can be signaled to others and to oneself. When it comes to the luxury industry, the race to the top *is* the race to the bottom.

48. The advent of big screen television also grabs your attention more than a smaller one because all the people portrayed on it are that much larger.

of the town. Players often played their entire careers for a single team and were fixtures in the civic life of the town. Fans' loyalty to their local team verged on the reverential. The fate of a team—think of the Chicago Cubs, who blundered their way through nine decades of championless seasons and into the hearts of professional sports lovers—not only bonded families, generations, and communities but strangers in bars and across the national landscape.

In the 21st century, baseball's role in communities has changed. To be fair, the change has come in the context of many changes in the game and in the country at large. The country is wealthier, yet the sport has also priced out many casual fans from spending a season with the team. Fan loyalty is not what it used to be, due to in large part to the increasing variety of entertainments available. It is also partly related to people relocating around the country for various reasons much more than they did in the past.

After Curt Flood challenged the reserve clause rule and opened the floodgates of free agency, players also began to relocate around the country at dizzying rates. It is not uncommon for a team's opening day roster to turn over 80 percent every five years. Since a player's identity is rarely tied to a town for more than a brief stint, fan adoration doesn't last much longer than a summer fling.

However, you would not sense this by looking at the numbers. Baseball attendance is near an all-time high, as are revenues. But ask one hundred kids in San Francisco today to name the starting lineup of their local team—one of the most storied franchises, which plays in a beautiful stadium that is packed nightly and wins championships with regularity—they probably could not name more than five players. That degree of apathy would have been unthinkable fifty years ago.

Let's go back to the evolutionary origins of sports. Ritualized, non-lethal competition is common among social species, and human social systems exhibit ritualized competitions that result in rank. Sorting rank through competition enables the development of dominance hierarchies that feed into secondary social behaviors, including rank-based mating, resource distribution, and cooperation. Evolution favors the emergence of such behaviors if they promote fitness from a multilevel selection perspective.

The evolutionary fitness value of physical prowess is probably less relevant in today's era, when humans gather resources more through proxies such as business success rather than hunting and gathering, but ritualized persistence of legacy behaviors is not uncommon in nature. It shouldn't be surprising that using success in sports to inform mating preference and resource distribution persists to this day.

But there's a deeper reason we are wired to give attention to sports: a tribal sense of affiliation. Given the change that matters most—those providing and participating in a sporting spectacle are no longer those who have kin skin in the game—the entire affair is becoming increasingly commoditized.

In the tribal era, our affiliation to competitors was likely high, given the kin skin in the game. In the era of the Roman Republic, however, fans' affiliation with the competitors was weak and competitions were attended more for the sense of spectacle than affiliation. In the Greek Republic, something different happened. The advent of the Olympics enabled fans to develop a sense of collective affiliation to teams and athletes based on characteristics other than kinship. Uniforms, insignias, and other markers of a shared identity were manufactured to replace relatedness as a basis for feeling kinship with a team.

In 19th-century America, a sense of collective affiliation began to develop toward teams and athletes based on what city one lived in and what university one attended. Thus the modern age of sports was spawned. As citizens grappled with an increasing sense of alienation and decreasing sense of community due to the replacement of high-aligned kin tribes with low-aligned communities of genetic strangers—sporting leagues were more than happy to provide an emotional salve of affiliation, however fleeting. It is perhaps not surprising that sports took off as a paid spectacle in the United States, where people felt the most distanced from the kin origins of human social evolution. They desperately needed to find common ground somewhere, somehow.

By the late 20th century, the success of collegiate and professional sports had allowed them to become major cultural institutions. A sense of affiliation among fans grew to the point of them becoming devotees who spend a disproportionate amount of time, attention, and resources on their sport of choice.

However, these sports' success at garnering attention and money led them to evolve ever more toward a commodification model. The relationship between players and fans became transactional as the industry treated it as one to be exploited for economic gain. Loyalty became a commodity to be sold and bartered. Every single part of the institution is for sale, from human bodies to stadium naming rights. At the beginning of the 21st century, collegiate and professional sports are bastardized versions of what they were a hundred years ago.

A sense of soullessness is usually a good barometer of whether an institution has turned into a low-alignment commodity. Instead of building a true sense of affiliation between athletes and fans, the business of sports is depleting the intangible values of a bygone era to maximize short-term gains while they last. Team owners will continue to flip ownership at ever higher prices until the music stops.

The declining sense of affiliation fans have with sports teams is evident to most people today. It has been replaced with a sense of the inevitability of the decline of the role collegiate and professional spectator sports play in people's lives. As with most institutions today, cynicism about sports is on the rise.

That is not to say the industry of spectator sports is about to collapse. There is still plenty of value left in the lore of the past and the roar of the current crowds. But it is important to recognize that the very soul of these games and institutions is at risk.

Youth Sports

At a time when the percentage of the national consciousness occupied by spectator sports is declining, another industry involving sports is rising: youth sports. In recent decades, youth sports has evolved from a rite of passage for kids into a rapidly burgeoning cottage industry that increasingly dominates the lives of families and communities. The peculiarities of modern youth sports culture are manifold, including the rise of club sports, and are extensively discussed in popular media today. For our purposes, we limit the discussion to the role of inclusive fitness in governing parents' behaviors related to youth sports culture.

From the broadest perspective, the disproportionate and increasing allocation of parents' attention, time, and resources to their children, instead of to community life, is entirely consistent with Hamilton's rule. People in modern lives have virtually no kin skin in the game in the lives of their neighbors. Thus, the fact that they put so much (arguably too much) effort and attention into their children is a reflection of the reality that their children are one of the only everyday receptacles for kin altruism in modern life. The network of uncles, aunts, cousins, and more distant relatives that dominated our prehistoric communities has been replaced by communities of genetic strangers. Thus, when it comes to community life, parents are putting all the eggs they fertilized into one basket—their own children—rather than into anything that remotely resembles the neighborhood life of years gone by. This behavior, which can come off as overzealous, in some ways is no different from the nepotism of imperial self-dealers.

Cue the "rug-rat race" among modern parents.[49]

The consequences are predictable within an evolutionary framework. First, families will be increasingly attracted to youth sports, especially club sports; the shared affiliation of youth sports fills the emotional void created by the destruction of the neighborhood sense of community. Indeed, families being drawn toward youth sports also draws them farther away from their physical neighbors, increasing the sense of neighborhood alienation that makes youth sports feel like an attractive alternative.

This is a feed-forward, self-fulfilling phenomenon. As fewer and fewer kids are available for free-range play in the home neighborhood, more and more families will surrender to joining youth sports where more and more kids are. Attending their kids' sporting events, including those that take them to remote locations, has become a pastime of parents to the exclusion of other social activities, including seeing one's spouse between Friday afternoon and Sunday evening. The youth sports industry is a self-expanding system with increasing premiums that need

49. See https://www.youtube.com/watch?v=KLlCv3Eb-mo.

to be paid to stay in the game. Those that can't afford these escalating fees are left behind, which adds to the economic and social division of communities.

Similarly, more and more families are relying on their kids' school communities for their social lives. In a time of increasing mobility and transactability, school has become one place where people can forecast the long duration of a committed membership that they feel is worth their investment of time and emotion. Parents' participation in school affairs at least partially reflects their sense of yearning to be part of any form of community.

This yearning is evident in the incessant use of the word "community" in modern life. In the past, people didn't need to use the word "community" because the sense was diffusely present. Today's overuse of the word is a market signal of a community that lacks a sense of community. The inverse relationship is evident in places like Silicon Valley, which uses the word "community" liberally but struggles to form strong ones.[50] People wave at each other with five fingers in their immediate neighborhood, with one finger during their commute, and with five fingers when they enter the drop off circle at their kids' schools.

The old sense of neighborhood is where the price is paid. The fact that many communities are made up people likely to move away at increasingly frequent rates fuels the lack of interest in investing in our neighbors' lives.

Absent a sense of community elsewhere in their lives, these children's games do matter emotionally to parents, the result being that too many parents spend too much time grooming their child to become high-status athlete. Again, Hamilton's rule prevails over all other social norms that we would wish for in a healthy social system.[51]

---

50. See https://www.mercurynews.com/2018/04/03/the-surprising-things-newcomers-love-and-hate-about-the-bay-area/.

51. Even within the context of the contrived sense of affiliation of belonging to a club team, Hamilton's rule is evident. Teams too often deal with infighting and jockeying for personal gain at the expense of others on the team. They are over-invested in what they perceive to be referee calls that go against their child and respond with a degree of aggression that would be unseemly in the context of a child's game.

Other Status Change Industries

There's a deeper story about why all competitions, not just sports, draw participants and spectators. Humans are innately wired to attune to not only status but status changes. If a status change is occurring within a social group, it has potential fitness import for the witnessing party. People can participate in contrived activities for the sake of amusement, wherein they experience status changes themselves or witness status changes in others. Such activities are the lure of games or sports, and participants may describe their experience as "fun" or "exciting," particularly when it involves status elevation, also known as "winning."

Our natural attentiveness to status changes has been exploited by the modern entertainment industry. A sport where the score is kept and a winner is declared is operating through status changes among participants. A football game might be called "great" if there are many lead changes (status changes) and "dramatic" if a status change occurs against all odds late in a game. A game where the underdog defeats the favored team might be perceived as "exciting" because of the unexpected status change. Indeed, we as consumers often demand that rank order be clarified for our own satisfaction and are willing to pay for that satisfaction.

Some people are addicted to checking score updates for their favorite teams. Others wake up on Monday morning and immediately check how the Top 25 college football rankings have changed since the previous week. Casey Kasem had a long-running weekly radio show on which the top 40 song rankings were updated. The most titillating moment of the hit television show American Idol occurs when a singer, whom the audience has been led to believe is of lower status, undergoes a status transformation while performing a single song. Downward status movement, such as when a celebrity hits a rough patch, also sells newspapers to a hungry public. The gossip industry is a status change industry.

The human mind seems voyeuristically drawn to undulating story lines of status change in books, plays, and movies. The mood changes in the scenes of Shakespeare's Romeo and Juliet can be described as alternating between low and high status: street brawl, intervention by the prince, Romeo mopes, meets Juliet, learns she's a Capulet, etc. Status change is considered a tool not only for drama or tragedy but for improvisational comedy, too.[52]

Facebook is many things to many people, but in many ways a Facebook page is a signaling device for status (or at least the commodification of information about status). How many friends we have, who our friends are, and what cool thing we did over the weekend are all status attributes. Every posting on the Facebook page changes our status relative to that of others. Indeed, the most powerful place in all of social media today is a box near the top of the Facebook page simply labeled, "status update."

Mortgage Lending

If you want to discuss the industry in which misaligned incentives have had the most disastrous economic impact in recent years, look no further than where you are right now. Chances are that the building you are in was affected by the 2007-2009 global meltdown of the real estate market.

As housing bubbles form, mortgage lending drifts toward risky loans, such as subprime lending, at exactly the least opportune time. Too often, lenders try to squeeze out the last of the profits of a boom period, knowing they will only partially bear the consequences if their loans default.

Indeed, after originating the loans, they can securitize them and sell them to secondary mortgage buyers at a small profit. The availability of these secondary markets ends up encouraging transactional behaviors. Buyers on the secondary market also hope to earn a small return, despite the risk the security carries. In many cases, they too flip loans like a hot potato. When the music stops (e.g., the housing market crashes) and defaults come into play, the people that made the decision to buy the mortgage-backed securities can walk away without paying much of a personal price, even though they gained from their decisions along the way.

---

52. See https://en.wikipedia.org/wiki/Keith_Johnstone.

Some of the losses from the housing crisis were borne by the banks and their shareholders. The bank executives pocketed the gains on the way up, and on the way down the losses were disproportionately borne by shareholders, borrowers, and the public. Moreover, the shareholders' decision to invest in banks often was made by investment managers who made money when bank share prices went up, and their clients bore the losses when share prices fell.

Taxpayers, too, were playing the same game. From a buyer's perspective, the risk and return are partially decoupled for home buyers in a way that promotes risk-taking. When housing prices rise, homeowners with mortgages keep the equity gains. Due to the non-recourse nature of many loans, when prices fall, homeowners can walk away and offload part or all of the losses onto the mortgage holders. During the housing bust of 2007-2009 and the subsequent rounds of government bailouts, many of the losses were passed onto Freddie Mac, Fannie Mae, or other financial institutions that had to be bailed out by the government. In other words, the home-buying public was partially able to socialize their losses.

It seems that individuals and corporations are able to benefit privately from profits and to push some of the losses onto others. This ability to at least partially offset the losses on the downside incentivizes depositors, homebuyers, money managers, banks, and corporations—in effect, every stakeholder—to take excess risk while chasing yield. The decoupling of risk from return invalidates many economic models, including the concept of the efficient frontier in modern port-folio theory, and forms a rather rational basis of irrational exuberance.[53] When the music stops, everyone passes the blame to someone else.

Everyone is pretty sure somebody else was responsible for the trillion-dollar real estate bust. No one ever admitted, "I did it." Not for a single buck of it.

---

53. See https://en.wikipedia.org/wiki/Modern_portfolio_theory; https://en.wikipedia.org/wiki/Effi-cient_frontier; the efficient frontier of modern portfolio theory relied on the assumption that investors make rational decisions according to expected risk and expected return. However, when people are able to capture the upside of an investment but socialize the losses, they tend to take excess risk in exchange for higher personal returns.

Buying a House

The principal-agent risk in a real estate transaction is an example of misaligned incentives. While there are regulations, government bodies that enforce licensing requirements, and industry education to mitigate the risk of a principal-agent problem, conflicts of interest still exist throughout the real estate industry.

To begin with the basics, a typical residential real estate transaction involves both a listing agent, who has a contract with the owner of the property up for sale, and a selling agent, who represents the buyer and negotiates on their behalf.[54] The agents, and their brokerage houses, split a 6 percent sales commission based on the price of the home sale.

At first glance, the interests of the seller-owner and the listing agent are aligned. The listing agent earns a percentage of the sales price as a fee. Looking deeper, however, trying to get the highest possible price for a home does more than increase the agent's fee: it increases the time the property lingers on the market and the probability that it may not sell at all.

For the listing agent, time is a valuable commodity, and seeking the highest possible price can reduce their overall sales productivity. Indeed, listing agents could net more income by increasing their sales volume, even if that means selling their listings at a lower price. This business reality conflicts with the interests of the seller-owner.

Many agents value their reputation and would not undersell the owner's interest for the sake of a quick sale. A good reputation also puts them in a position to earn repeat business and referrals.

But the long-term relationship between agents and clients in residential real estate are somewhat tenuous. A typical client may be involved in a handful of transactions over a lifetime, many of which will involve relocating outside the

---

54. The selling agent is colloquially referred to as the "buying agent." Go figure.

area of an agent's expertise. From a client's perspective, maintaining loyalty with a particular agent may or may not pay off.

More telling is how brokerages reward listing and selling agents. Treasured metrics in the industry are sales volume and total dollars. The primary barrier to growing these metrics is the bid-ask spread between the home buyer and seller. Thus, a latent motivation of the listing agent is to lower the seller's price expectation, and a latent motivation of the selling agent (a.k.a. buying agent) is to raise the buyer's price expectation.

All of this is well and good, except that the fiduciary obligation of a listing agent generally is to sell the property for the owner at the highest possible price, while accounting for the seller's tolerance for time the property lingers on the market. And the fiduciary duty of the selling agent (a.k.a. the buying agent) generally is to acquire the desired property at the lowest possible price.

On the one hand, agents can defend their actions that drive toward narrowing the bid-ask spread. The seller wants to sell and the buyer wants to buy. But for their clients, as with all negotiated transactions, there is a tradeoff between getting the deal done and getting the deal done at the best price. Agents' economic incentive to drive that bid-ask spread to zero can get in the way of serving the latter objective.

The cozy relationships between buying and selling agents amplify this risk. Dual agency represents one of the most troubling examples of the principal-agent problem in real estate transactions. In dual agency, a single agent represents the buyer and seller of a property, which puts the fiduciary obligation to each party in direct conflict with the interests of the seller and buyer.

The cozy relationships between real estate agents and transaction vendors also pose risks to the clients. In most cases, the agents refer the vendors to the buyers and sellers. Given the lure of earning repeat referrals from agents, vendor incentives are more aligned with the referring agents than their actual clients. Thus, they may be incentivized to underplay information that would reduce the likelihood of a deal closing and overplay information that increases the likelihood of the deal closing. The liability risk of this strategy is mitigated by preemptive disclaimers.

All of these incentive issues are ironically embedded in the words real estate, whose original meaning is "to have an interest in the thing." If only this "thing" could be the best interest of clients.

CHAPTER SIX

Stampede of Self-Expanding Beasts

The above examples of race-to-the-bottom-line incentives structures are hardly exhaustive. Even housing comes out looking like a paradise of aligned incentives when compared with the perversity of the U.S. healthcare system. It suffices to Google "opioid epidemic" for an indication of the litany of misaligned incentives that plagues the industry.[55] Marx claimed that religion was "the opiate of the masses"; today, tragically, opiates are the religion of the masses.

Indeed, virtually every institutional category, to one extent or another, is similarly undermined by perverse incentives. The purpose of this book is not to catalogue them all. We are merely using the cited examples across disparate industries to focus on the higher-level meta-observations.

Looking across the entire landscape of institutions, the race to the bottom line is neither a purely corporate illness nor an affliction of the most selfish and greediest among us. Rather, it is a structural condition affecting every institutional category in society: human social institutions have consistently exhibited a tendency to evolve from high-minded, high-alignment origins to self-dealing, low-alignment maturity. As Harvard evolutionary biologist Joseph Henrich notes in The Secret of Our Success,[56] all pro-social institutions collapse over time at the hands of self-interest.

Each generation and each category of institutions we have described— across the broad sweep of history in Part I and across the landscape of society in

---

55. See https://www.nytimes.com/2018/10/11/nyregion/doctors-charged-opioid-prescriptions.html; https://www.amazon.com/Dreamland-True-Americas-Opiate-Epidemic/dp/1511336404.
56. See https://press.princeton.edu/titles/10543.html.

Part II—did not start out with the intention of self-dealing and racing to the bottom line. Yet, in every instance, from the Roman gladiators endorsing olive oil to the pharmaceutical industry marketing opiates, self-dealing and corruption have been the outcome. Why is that? Were the pioneers who led the institutional revolutions we have described inadequately virtuous? Did they attack the beasts of inequality and injustice with inadequate zeal?

Obviously not. In social systems as much as in biological ones, an individual virtue or failing is no match for evolutionary pressures.

Ever since humanity set out on the long march of progress that has lifted us from hunter-gatherer subsistence to today's urbanized abundance and material bliss, we have been seeking to re-create or create new versions of incentive systems that we left behind: the natural kin skin in the game alignment that came from our life in kin tribes.

Put differently, for tens of thousands of years we have been trying to get home to the place where our moms, dads, cousins, uncles, and aunts cooked our meals and were our heroes. That is the world our reptilian brains expect when we wake up every morning. That is the world our reptilian brains believe we walk into every day. And time after time—whether we have awoken in Babylon or Brooklyn or whether we have set out in golden raiments or Gore-Tex parkas—we are disappointed to find that the institutions we trusted did not have our best interests in mind.

Earlier, we described how increased social entropy was the first-order phenom-enon that led to second-order phenomena such as the reduced alignment of inter-est and increased relationship liquidity. These issues contributed to third-order phenomena, which we summarized as evolutionary maladaptation of the social, political, and economic behaviors of institutions and individuals. The race to the bottom line was a fourth-order phenomenon.

We now describe a set of fifth-order phenomena: the Race to the Middle, the Byzantine Reflex, and the Self-Expanding Beast.

The Race to the Middle

Is the race to the bottom bottomless? Aren't races supposed to end?

Maybe.

If a race to the bottom becomes egregious, a revolt led by the exploited can overthrow the establishment. At least that view is often served up as a temporary salve, however fleeting, for the plague of races to the bottom everywhere.

The possibility of revolt, including those in which heads end up on the chopping block, is evident to those in power. Thus, to some extent, the oppressors have a vested interest in putting the brakes on a runaway race to the bottom, not because they have a sense of justice but to save their own necks. Even in this situation, the power of vested self-interest is at work.

For those in political power, concessions—including term limits and a system of checks and balances—put the brakes on the self-reinforcing, race-to-the-bottom nature of that power. For those with economic power, concessions—including progressive taxation, philanthropy, and virtue signaling[57]—put the brakes on the self-reinforcing, race-to-the-bottom nature of wealth inequality. If a revolt is necessary, some of the empowered may even take the side of the revolutionaries for a wide variety of stated and actual reasons.

What this means is that many races to the bottom eventually correct course to become a race to the middle. In some ways, the race to the middle is worse than the race to the bottom, as it deters institutional cleansing of latent corruption. On the other hand, the race to the middle has generally helped guide the trajectory of human life upwards, lifting all boats.

The race to the middle is a curse and a gift—a theme we will return to again.

---

57. See https://en.wikipedia.org/wiki/Virtue_signalling.

The Byzantine Reflex

Once an organization or an institution gains power, it has a natural incentive to protect that power and the status quo.[58] In medieval times, such protection might have taken the form of a castle topped with battlements and surrounded by a moat. Modern-day institutions exhibit not only updated versions of a moat but a subtler approach like the one Dame Gothel employs to hide Rapunzel in the Grimm fairy tale: a deliberately cultivated thicket.

Industrial economists understand well the tendency of powerful incumbents to use their influence on governments to construct elaborate "regulatory thickets" that inhibit competitive challenge. However, the phenomenon is very general. In monarchical eras, courtesans similarly constructed elaborate, almost impenetrable rituals to protect their positions of influence and power. The phrase "Byzantine complexity" refers to the impossibly complicated protocols and procedures of the Byzantine Empire, which was the continuation of the Roman Empire in its eastern provinces in late antiquity.[59] However, the infamous rituals of the Byzantine court were exceptionally complex only in comparison with the norms of the era, when most monarchs were elevated feudal lords and royal courts were relatively rough-hewn affairs.

While most of the complexity that allows modern exchange economies to exist is deeply submerged in digital protocols and, increasingly, nearly inscrutable machine learning algorithms, enough remains on the surface to make the Byzantine court look like a family affair. This is not because complexity tends to increase within any institution over time (as was largely true of the Byzantine Empire) but because powerful incumbents have learned to use complexity as a barrier against competition.

---

58. This is also true within the "bureaucracy of the mind" that lives inside each of our brains.
59. "Guests at royal banquets were assigned titles that denoted where they could sit in relation to the emperor, whom they could talk to, and what they were allowed to discuss. Eventually, the rituals became so complex that treatises were written to help outsiders understand proper etiquette, and the emperor employed officials to teach newbies how to behave." See https://slate.com/news-and-politics/2011/10/the-byzantine-tax-code-how-complicated-was-byzantium-anyway.html.

The Byzantine Reflex refers to systems that are characterized by a tendency to self-evolve toward greater complexity and obfuscation in a way that favors the asymmetric beneficiaries of the status quo. Indeed, such systems will self-select against simplicity and transparency. A corrupt government will do nothing to stop complicating government regulations since such obfuscations enable them to set predatory traps on the public.

The American healthcare system is a current case in point. In every dimension of the healthcare system, a natural progression toward the Byzantine is evident as the system evolves to avoid transparency and accountability.

The take home point is this: unless there is alignment of interest to protect you from abuses, in any system that contains Byzantine complexity, be wary of an underlying counterparty that could be acting against your interest.

Self-Expanding Beasts

The race to the bottom line and the Byzantine Reflex naturally produce a world in which the institutional clusters that gain market dominance are pressured toward ever-increasing scale and reach. Having exhausted all the naturally occurring inputs to growth, the systems naturally evolve to generate false needs and artificial demand.

The product of the healthcare system is not healthcare but old people who need more healthcare. Big Food produces fake news about fake foods that increases demand for more fake food. The product of the media is ignorance and confusion, which creates a demand for more media.

For the purposes of this book, any self-dealing institution or system that was designed to serve the people but has mutated to serve itself by exploiting the people will hereby be referred to as a "beast."

Any institution that has self-engineered runaway feedback loops in its favor (and at the expense of the people) will hereby be referred to as a "self-expanding beast." In a race-to-the-bottom world, the system selects for the beasts that are the best at self-expansion—that is, the worst actors—by crowding out less malignant beasts.

By the way, this is essentially how a colony of cancer cells operates.

Here's how self-expanding beasts feed their own growth. As just noted, the current healthcare system—at the end of the day, and at the "end of our days"— creates old people. That is, the more successful the healthcare system is at helping people live longer without solving the problem of aging, the older the population becomes. An aging population needs and pays for more healthcare, which expands the balance sheet of healthcare companies. These companies in turn use the balance sheet for more development and marketing.

Similarly, the more consumers feed on clickbait news and drink high-fructose, corn-syrup-flavored drinks, the more they empower the very companies that are exploiting them. The self-dealing media and food companies in turn get richer and are able to spend more dollars to bait consumers, forming a vicious cycle. In essence, these companies turn into self-expanding beasts that grow ever larger at the expense of the people. Growth is the dominant imperative of these beasts: the greater their capacity to self-feed, the greater their capacity to grow.

Yet, if anything, we seem to be falling in love with our captors as if afflicted with Stockholm syndrome.

Our modern love affairs with institutions could be traced back to the publication in 1651 of Leviathan, Thomas Hobbes' masterwork of political philosophy. In Leviathan, Hobbes famously describes the dog-eat-dog reality of human existence in the absence of political communities of various types:

In such condition, there is no place for industry; because the fruit thereof is uncertain: and consequently no culture of the earth; no navigation, nor use of the commodities that may be imported by sea; no commodious building; no instruments of moving, and removing, such things as require much force; no knowledge of the face of the earth; no account of time; no arts; no letters; no society; and which is worst of all, continual fear, and danger of violent death; and the life of man, solitary, poor, nasty, brutish, and short.[60]

60.   Malcolm, N. (2012). *Leviathan*. Oxford, UK: Oxford University Press.

Given that, when Hobbes wrote these words, the homicide rate in Europe was about ten times what it is today and life expectancy was about half, it may seem a bit surprising that Hobbes would draw any favorable contrast at all between his era and preceding ones. But Hobbes was one of the first major figures of the English Enlightenment, and he wrote at the very beginning of a remarkable era of social and economic transformation. Along multiple irrefutable dimensions, our lives today are dramatically better not only than those of our distant relations who lived in kin tribes but also than the contemporaries of Thomas Hobbes.

So what's the problem?

The French existentialists had it partly right when they pointed to the "alienation" of modern man. Compared to our ancestors, we modern humans are systematically disconnected—alienated, if you will—from our neighbors, the natural world around us, our leaders, the food we eat … pretty much anything but our pets and the success of our children, both of which have become the subject of almost unbounded attention and investment.

However, alienation is a passive term that does not capture the active misalignment of interests that have been the focus of Part II. Institutions in a race-to-the-bottom-line world evolve into self-expanding beasts in a purposeful, incentive-driven process.

It is evident that diaspora/social entropy/trying to coexist with each other in low-alignment communities is inherently fraught with issues. Our factory setting is biased toward exploiting strangers (reciprocal altruism) and trusting kin (kin altruism). Furthermore, reciprocal altruism has a flaw; it assumes that both sides have insight. In reality, information asymmetry, as well as hard-wired preferences (attraction to porn, violence, sugar, gossip), can be mined. Moreover, the feed-forward nature of the growth of these self-expanding beasts allows them to invest in better ways to increase and exploit asymmetries.

If you take a step back and look around, you'll see that such self-expanding beasts are everywhere in modern society.

CHAPTER SEVEN

Solidarity and "Solitarity"

Selfish behavior is not an affliction limited to institutions. Rather, it affects virtually every corner of life today. It has a way of feeding upon itself. In this chapter, we discuss the shift of the ethos of human communities from the solidarity of tribes to the "solitarity" of modern living.

Solidarity is the unity of a group based on common interests, objectives, standards, and sympathies.[61] It refers to the ties in a society that bind people as one.[62] Solitarity, on the other hand, is the state of being alone.[63] The two words are antonyms that together help explain the existence of an individual's concurrent and often competing interests and values at any moment in time. Together, they help us understand the path of history—evolutionarily, socially, and culturally—that we have been on over time.

Historically, the study of social systems often has assumed that evolution proceeds from a solitary state to a social one.[64] Recent phylogenetic studies of bees contradict this assumption. In the evolution of social systems, descendants of an altruistic eusocial group can evolve back to solitary behavior once again—a phenomenon known as reversal to solitarity or secondary solitarity.[65] Eusociality

61. See https://www.merriam-webster.com/dictionary/solidarity.
62. See https://en.wikipedia.org/wiki/Solidarity.
63. See https://en.wikipedia.org/wiki/Eusociality.
64. See https://www.sciencedirect.com/science/article/pii/S0169534797011981.
65. See https://www.sciencedirect.com/science/article/pii/S0169534797011981.

in bees is thought to have evolved at least four times, and reversal of a species to solitarity is thought to have occurred at least nine separate times.[66] A reversal to solitarity has been described in other animals as well.[67]

On the one hand, reversal to solitarity suggests that eusociality may be costly to sustain and that it is evolutionarily selected against when the adaptive context no longer favors it. One example of such a disadvantage is the vulnerability of the entire lineage of a kin tribe to infectious epidemics. On the other hand, changing the strategies of a social system is evolutionarily costly, so these strategies exhibit self-stability.[68]

Human social systems are evolutionarily wired for a bygone era when kin-based, hive-like tribal behaviors were favored. It's possible that humans are headed to become the tenth known example of a species in the animal kingdom evolving from a social system of solidarity to one of solitarity (one driven far more by individual self-interest than interpersonal interests, as discussed in Chapter 3). On the evolutionary time scale, however, the biologic code underlying human social systems has not been able to adapt as fast as the changing ecological context, including cultural and technological changes of our own making. Specifically, human social behaviors that were wired for a highly aligned social system can operate maladaptively when the evolutionary dislocation created by modern technology puts humans in a position where they have to coexist in low-aligned communities.

It would take a very long time for the evolution of the biological code under-lying human social systems to revert to one that is well adapted to solitarity. And yet, the cultural changes that have occurred at breathtaking speed relative to biological evolution and have resulted in highly frequent transactions among genetic strangers demand more immediate shifts in human social behavior. These

66.   Gadagkar, R. (1993). "And now... eusocial thrips!" *Current Science,* 64, 215-216; Michener, C. D. (1969). Comparative social behavior of bees. *Annual Review of Entomology,* 14, 299-342.
67.   See https://www.sciencedirect.com/science/article/pii/S0169534797011981; https://en.wikipedia. org/wiki/Eusociality#Reversal_to_solitarity.
68.   Shell, W. A., & Rehan, S. M. (2017). Behavioral and genetic mechanisms of social evolution: Insights from incipiently and facultatively social bees. *Apidologie,* 49, 1-18.

shifts in the genetic code will not happen soon, and nor it is evident that such shifts would prove beneficial in the long run.

In the meantime, the lag error between modern cultural evolution and our biological factory settings—a fundamental evolutionary maladaptation—has produced millennia of dysfunction (where individual self-interest trumps interpersonal interests) at the operating-system level of human society. As noted in prior chapters, the response at this level has been awkward at best and self-destructive at worst.

Or, at least, so it seems.

An epiphenomenon of the drift of prevailing social behaviors from kin selection to self-dealing is the cultural emergence of the "self movement." In some ways, this movement has become the most significant self-expanding beast of all.

Here's why.

Self-dealing as a social phenomenon has a way of feeding upon itself in a self-reinforcing loop. As people feel betrayed by or alienated from others, they begin to self-deal. In so doing, they alienate others, further propagating the vicious cycle. In every case, that "other" is "ourselves."[69]

In kin tribes of yore, we balanced taking personal responsibility with taking responsibility for each other. Today, relationships are more transactional. Following Hamilton's rule, our reptilian brain executes the default setting by taking less responsibility for those around us so we can focus more personal responsibility on ourselves.

What results is a self-expanding cult of the self movement. In such a system, the marketplace for psychology neologisms selects its own self-expanding taxonomy. Words that once involved a second person are now used increasingly to describe first-person concepts. Advocacy used to mean speaking up for others, and schools now teach self-advocacy. Mindfulness used to mean being mindful

---

69. We are each other's counterparties. Our behaviors are mirror images of each other's.

of others, but now it is part of a self-help, personal-enrichment movement.[70] We live in a world with self-service stations and take self-guided tours where we take selfies. Reliance involved a second person until Ralph Waldo Emerson launched the self-reliance movement in 1841.[71] Help used to involve a second person until George Combe inaugurated the self-help movement in 1829.[72] No wonder that, despite being connected to more people than ever, we've never felt more alienated and alone. As a result, the echo chamber of the Internet inevitably concludes that the most important thing is to love yourself—which could not be more distant from the Socratic admonition to "know thyself."

The self-help movement exemplifies the self-expanding nature of self-movement beasts. In the book marketplace, imagine trying to sell a book about helping others, being mindful of others, advocating for others, and taking responsibility for others. Such books would find a limited audience (except for religious books—more on that later), so authors tend not to write them and publishers tend not to publish them.

What do sell—the literary litter that self-dealing, self-aggrandizing authors and publishers are willing to create—are self-help books. Next time you go to a bookstore, marvel at how large the self-help section is and how much it has grown during your lifetime. Compare it to the size of the "help-others section" of the bookstore.

"What 'help-others' section?" you might well ask.

Exactly.

People have been memetically primed to buy self-help books. The publishing industry is more than happy to profit from selling into this memetic channel, thereby expanding their own balance sheet and market power. Authors and the publishing industry organize around the value system of self-dealing by selling more self-help books, and so on. Self-promotion becomes the engine that feeds itself through the publishing ecosystem.

---

70. See https://www.amazon.com/Remarks-Delivered-2017-Purpose-Awards-ebook/dp/B0763JW4YH/.
71. See https://en.wikipedia.org/wiki/Self-Reliance.
72. See https://en.wikipedia.org/wiki/Self-help.

Of course, there is no transparency in this particular truth. As with all self-expanding beasts, incentives and rewards are self-organized in a way that obscures the reality in order to protect itself—the aforementioned Byzantine Reflex.

In the competitive race to the bottom, in order to sell more books, self-help books have to scream louder and louder about the degree of self-advocacy that one should practice.[73] Eventually, it becomes about the screaming itself. Victimhood and self-righteous marches ensue.

In other words, like the Kardashians and high-fructose corn syrup, the system self-selects for the most egregious violations of what would actually be helpful.

The emergence of modern psychology is another epiphenomenon of the self movement.

In the 19th century, the industrial and scientific revolutions had finally given us the leisure time and tools to create modern psychology as a formal field of study. The first International Congress of Psychology took place in Paris in 1889, and the American Psychological Association was founded soon thereafter.[74]

For the most part, we spent the ensuing century gazing at where we came from—our umbilical stumps. Sigmund Freud helped us explore the concept of ego, and Abraham Maslow identified self-actualization as the most advanced human need.[75] Today, virtually absent from the field of psychology is the psychology of "other." There is little interest in the opportunity to extend psychology beyond the first-person perspective.

But surely, you say, isn't the modern interest in empathy a sign that we are interested in being mindful of others? The short answer is, yes. It's a great start.

However, let's unpack the empathy movement further. The word empathy is defined as the capacity to understand what another person is experiencing from

---

73. The system selects for fake stories with fake relevance for the reader.
74. See https://en.wikipedia.org/wiki/Psychology.
75. See https://en.wikipedia.org/wiki/Maslow%27s_hierarchy_of_needs.

within the frame of reference of another person. It was coined by E. B. Titchener in 1909 as the translation of the German term einfühlung (or "feeling into").

Before you get too far down the road of wondering what the heck we were thinking in the ten thousand years of conscious human history before the word empathy was finally coined, consider that, even today, there is no word to denote the feeling of "seeking empathy."

Humans tend to desire empathy from others. We can intuit that the empathy-giving trait co-evolved with an empathy-seeking trait as twin adaptations to promote social evolution. Yet we've only come around to naming half of the pair.

Meanwhile, interest in the science of empathy continues to grow rapidly. Scientists use tools like functional magnetic resonance imaging to scan the brain for the neurological basis of empathy. Curiously, scholars neglect the science of those seeking empathy. Why?

If an empathizer is someone who empathizes, what term describes the recipient of empathy—empathee? In a perverse irony, scientists and linguists who study empathy but overlook the would-be recipient of empathy may exemplify a lack of empathy.[76]

Finally, "understanding what another person is experiencing" says nothing about what the empathizer intended to do with that piece of understanding. Does the empathizer intend to use that information on behalf of the empathee or on behalf of their own self-interest? One outcome of the Internet age is that many institutions know more about people than people know about themselves. They are data-gathering machines masquerading as service industries (without naming names, think of virtually every fast-growing technology, media, social media, app, e-commerce company of the past decade). They use and sell that data to maximize their own economic gain at the expense of the people.[77]

Empathy is merely a tool. Like all tools, it can be used to serve others or abuse others. The tool is not inherently the problem; the intent is. The most important question is, whom does it serve?

---

76. See https://www.amazon.com/Hiding-Plain-Sight-Essays-Joon-ebook/dp/B019NH70YE/.
77. Unlike your mom, these companies put their own interests first, instead of yours.

For modern psychology—first-person psychology—the answer, so far, is that it serves the self movement.

Selfhood implies a first-person perspective.[78] In doing so, it tautologically creates otherhood as an epiphenomenon. The feed-forward nature of the self movement, then, expands the gulf between self and other. Separatism is thus a self-expanding concept. Furthermore, since self-dealing is the inherent intent of the self movement, it is inevitable that assign what we perceive to be desirable qualities to our ego and assign the less desirable qualities to others.[79]

The separatism of hero and anti-hero archetypes is an inevitable emergent property of the self movement. As a matter of existential convenience, people generally prefer to identify with the hero archetype. In doing so, we can also conveniently dump all the burdens on the various anti-hero "beasts" (internal and external) that our therapists, coaches, and gurus will incite us to attack and slay.

One notable example in this category is Joseph Campbell's idea of the "Hero's Journey." He described the Hero's Journey as the story of individuals who, through great suffering, reach an experience of the eternal source and return with the means to set their society free. Typically, a person leaves home on an adventure, slays a beast, and returns home to close a journey of transformation and redemption.[80]

A couple of features of the Hero's Journey are worth mentioning. The first was highlighted by Campbell himself. In The Hero with a Thousand Faces, he

---

78. Self-hood implies a first-person perspective.
79. We will later discuss our tendency to split the universe (a word that literally means "one story") in two by separating it into a black and white story. "That [the narrator of Genesis] transferred the impulse to temptation outside man was almost more a necessity for the story than an attempt at making evil something existing outside man"; von Rad, G. (1973). *Genesis: A commentary* (rev. ed.). Philadelphia: The Westminster Press, pp. 87-88. Later, in the spirit of recursive duality, we discuss how the original sin is the original gift. In the spirit of recursive duality, we will contradict ourselves and note that the commodified version of Genesis, which protects Man from realizing he is part good and part bad, was a gift and not a sin. Thus, the expulsion from Eden was actually a launch. The ambiguity of this concept is both its curse and its gift.
80. In other variations, such as Dickens' "A Christmas Carol" (subtitled "Being a Ghost Story of Christmas") and Frank L. Baum's *The Wonderful Wizard of Oz*, it is not entirely clear if any physical displacement actually occurs in the course of the Hero's Journey. Beasts (or, in Dorothy's case, a pair of witches) are encountered and (again in Dorothy's case) slain in one or another transient, mythical land, but the true journey is internal. The hero returns home, but in fact the hero has never left. The beast that was overcome, and

makes the case that the Hero's Journey is a monomyth that comprises the vast panoply of enduring stories, stretching back to ancient epics and the Bible itself.

The second feature to be highlighted is more insidious. The consolidated and appealing narrative of a person whose life journey is to become the hero and be transformed as a person is another instantiation of the self movement. It is, quite possibly, the hubris of narcissism at its zenith, and a natural extension of Freud's concept of ego and Maslow's concept of self-actualization.

One could make the case that the sum total of all the Hero's Journeys in the world has gotten us exactly to the point we occupy as a society today, as described elsewhere in the book. What if our obsession with being the hero, slaying the beast, and being transformed is a central contributor to our current dystopia? What if our obsession with our own journey, heroic and otherwise, is itself "a self-expanding beast" of the type we described above?

There's probably a reason why this so-called monomyth has needed an endless series of sequels, each commanding ever higher fees for those on the production side. Their enduring appeal speaks to the possible reality that the need for that story to be retold is only growing, possibly a result of its own success.

What if we—all of us, manifesting our most heroic "kill the beast" selves—are at the core of the very problem we are trying to solve?

the power to return home was with the hero all along.

CHAPTER EIGHT

Duality and Separatism

So how do we turn the tide on the epidemic of selfish behaviors that have corroded our institutions and eroded our communities? We believe the first step is to bust the central myth of the past few millennia: that there is a separation between good and evil people in the world.

In the real world, individuals are not either good or evil. We are all both good and evil. There are no groups of heroes versus beasts. There are no groups of white knights versus black nights. Everyone has polarities as well as shades of grey. Everyone harbors both the yin and the yang. It's a truth that's neither palatable to the ego nor marketable for those that want to sell a story.

Yet, this duality is the reality.

———————

At the end of the day, everyone participates in the greater system in a way that causes some harm to others, however subtle or remote, but there is a general blindness to this reality. Our minds tend to downplay our role in the harm that we cause others and overplay the role of others in the harm we experience.

In the preceding chapters, we mentioned that self-expanding, race-to-the-bottom beasts are everywhere—in the food we eat, the social networks we track, the pills we take, the sports teams we follow, the political machines we support, and the self-help groups we join. What we miss—nearly all of us, nearly all of the time—is something more fundamental: that all of these self-dealing, race-to-the-bottom organizations have grown out of the same global petri-dish of misaligned incentives that is modernity. And all of them feed on the same set of primal instincts that allowed us to survive prehistory.

What's notable is that we have little trouble seeing the evil in others. We easily recognize them and call them out in the institutions of which we are not a part. Corporate executives and entrepreneurs have no difficulty recognizing the self-dealing beast that is government bureaucracy; noble civil servants (a.k.a. government bureaucrats) have similarly little difficulty recognizing the self-dealing beasts on Wall Street and in Silicon Valley. Pulitzer Prize-winning news organizations understand that their duty is to reveal the self-dealing beast that is the political system. Politicians assert that it is their duty to reveal the fundamental corruption of the media.

The general blindness to this reality is evidenced by Goodwin's Law, the Internet rule asserting that, "as an online discussion grows longer, the probability of a comparison involving Nazis or Hitler approaches 1." Importantly, this law holds regardless of the characteristics or the views of the individuals engaged in such discussions. It evidences the fact that our society has evolved (or cultivated) a deep-seated need to experience not only as evil but as absolute evil all those who oppose our many and varied heroic quests.

We all gaze across the moats that divide us and point to the self-dealing beasts on the other side. We Occupy. We Tea Party. We Yellow Jacket. We sue. We counter-sue and counter-counter-sue. We Tweet, we post. Above all, we attack. We do so fueled by the conviction that the wind of history is behind us.

Yet, even if we were to prevail in demolishing all the beasts we perceive around us, we would be seen as the beast by others who want to take us down.

And so it is that we proceed on seven billion Hero's Journeys that add up to single collective ride on the Carousel of History.

The following story offers a further illustration of how hard it is to detect our role in the suffering of others.

We have a labradoodle puppy. He is descended from a lineage of canines that hunted and killed for their meals. He harbors a dog-eat-dog past—we all did—but lives in a dog-eat-dog-food present. He's been bred and domesticated to be friendly, furry, pettable, and even hypoallergenic for my allergy-prone dad; he definitely has not been bred for his ability to hunt. He couldn't hurt most creatures if he tried. If he started eating what he killed, we'd probably give him away. His benign nature is the reason we didn't keep the receipt when we brought him home.

That's not to say that the killing has stopped. He is eating dog food made from living creatures that were killed out of sight by "the machine." "The machine" is probably one of those self-expanding beasts that profit from a system that we feed with our purchases. What about humans? Are we dog-eat-dog people, or we are good innocent people who bask in the illusion of domesticated bliss while displacing the "evil" onto a system that we disparage but nonetheless feed into (and thus are a part of)?

By and large, we have chosen the latter narrative. Rather than accepting our total identity—that each of us is simultaneously the beast and the hero, the good and the evil, the problem and the solution—we have chosen, through memetic parallax, to segregate these identities. We have chosen to believe in the myth of separatism.

In separatism, we identify ourselves as the good people. We identify the opposing side as inherently bad people. If we think the other team is the good team, we switch sides. To that bad team we assign the role of monsters, beasts, legendary creatures, and the devil, all the while being blind to the possibility that we too might have a beastly side. We are blind to the fact that the other side sees us as the monsters.

We are both good and evil but find it difficult to accept that duality.

—————————

In many ways, our sociality has been devolving from where we started. Over time we have abandoned the reality of duality in favor of separatism. Our worsening blindness stems in no small part from the myths we hold on to.

In the story of Eden, there's a serpent with no prior allegorical ontogenesis (more on this character later) who seduces Eve, who then seduces Adam. Adam and Eve then consume a forbidden apple from the Tree of Knowledge. Our first ancestors' disobedience and expulsion from Eden led to our awareness of the separateness of good and evil.

An outcome of separatism is the construction and expansion of the concept of self, the ego. This speaks to the possibility that the self movement has been going on for a long time.

Maybe leaving the hearth of our kin tribe marked the beginning of time as we know it. Maybe time was timeless in the Eden of kin tribes. As the kin tribe connections slowly disintegrated and our sociality devolved, instead of time just being current, it started moving upstream against the current—the journey to a savage inward darkness. More and more, we acted against, instead of for, the interests of others.

Within a nuclear family, the human experience is characterized by unconditional love, service, and sacrifice. For nearly everyone in the nuclear family, these behaviors are programmed and promoted by the 50 percent genetic vested interest they have in each other. While the husband and wife are not typically genetically related to one another, they share the aforementioned reproductive bioprogramming and mutually vested genetic interest in their progeny that promotes love, service, fairness, and sacrifice.

Over the generations, however, the shared genetic vested interest is diluted more quickly than you might realize. Grandchildren have ¼ of their genes in common, great-grandchildren only ⅛. After ten generations, the degree of genetic correlation among descendants is as low as 0.0009. In other words, they are genetic strangers.[81] Assuming twenty years between generations, the original nuclear family spawns a network of strangers in a short two hundred years.

Among strangers who lack kin skin in the game, self-dealing instincts mathematically overwhelm kin altruistic instincts. Some collaborative behaviors among strangers (e.g., the reciprocal altruism or conditional love among friends) can create bonds. However, it's the extractive, nefarious, and even predatory behaviors among strangers that cast a shadow over the human experience. Where that

---

81.   Different cultures have different standards as to what the border is between stranger and relative.

breakpoint occurs is a matter of circumstance. On the one hand, there's fratricide, when the downstream stakes motivate that behavior. On the other hand, there's philanthropy for genetic strangers on other continents. The most important point here is that, starting from the original house, vested interest between nuclear families declines over the generations even as the vested interest within nuclear families stays intact.

From the point of view of any one person, the contrast between altruistic behaviors among kin groups and transactional behaviors among strangers is readily apparent. We all start with the original experience of our mother's unconditional love in utero, and later experience the extractive behavior of strangers. We first become aware of light when we exit the tunnel of unconditional love. From that moment forward we become increasingly aware of duality.

That moment is worth a good cry.

To some extent, the stress of dealing with strangers is diffused by forces of mutual repulsion. Diaspora is typically couched in a lovely story of families adventuring forward, but it's not unequally motivated by the dispersion instinct propelled by the stress of dealing with low-aligned relatives. Take one's nuclear family and hit the road.

The broader point is that people become aware of good behaviors and bad behaviors. It is at this point we slip into a fallacy.

We tend to group behaviors into two disparate clusters and build simplistic, black-and-white archetypes. It is as if one thing embodies all the evil and the other thing embodies all the good. Once these archetypes have been sculpted, creating stories is fairly trivial. Think of all the stories we've told ourselves and each other about monsters, legendary creatures, hobbits, trolls, devils, angels, heroes, and gods. It's not only trivial…it's unstoppable.

We, of course, tend to think of ourselves as the heroes fighting against the bad guys. If we pay closer attention to reality, we observe something different. The most evil self-dealing Wall Street crook did it for the unconditional love of his kids. The most evil self-dealing monarch did it to give the kingdom to his beloved kids. As we self-righteously judge the evil behaviors of strangers while showing unconditional love for our own children, we are blind to the fact that we are the self-dealing stranger that others judge.

The disdain is mutual. So is the self-flattery. We can see each other's hypocrisies but be blind to our own.

In reality, we are all mixed parts of good and bad, yet something made us see the world in black and white, made us believe that there are separate heroes and monsters. And something made us believe that we are the heroes. What made us believe that?

It was the stories we've told ourselves.

Was duality—that notion we each embody both good and evil—the "original" story before it was displaced by the modern myth of separatism?

At the beginning of this book, we praised parental love. Then we chafed at the nepotism it spawned. We then lauded competition for shaping prosperity. Then we impugned it for creating a world in which we gorge on high-fructose corn syrup and the Kardashians. You can feel the tension of these self-contradictions. In one minute, an institution is the hero in our story. In the next, it is the beast we are attacking. The distinction between hero and beast comes across indistinctly at best.

No concept embodies the tension inherent in this duality better than the Chinese taijitu symbol of yin and yang. Yin and yang beautifully express both symmetry and opposition. The mutuality of yin and yang is dynamic, with each force begetting the other in a never-ending cycle. According to the philosophy represented by the yin and yang symbol, all aspects of existence flows from this cycle of opposing forces, including flow itself.

Independence and interdependence are the yin and yang of human coexistence. Neither extreme can stake a claim as the optimum modality for human sociality.

Based on yin and yang, we should be at the forefront of the rise of contrecoup forces—a swing back to tribalism as a rejection of the hug of globalization (an embrace which is increasingly being performed with knives held behind backs).

The countercultural swing back to tribalism would restore balance. But does that mean it's a good thing? If it's meant to be a good thing, it sure doesn't feel that way. Deep fractures seem to appear daily today along every tribal element of human identity: gender, race, geography, wealth, age, and politics. As in some apocalyptic action movies, we hardly know where to step in day-to-day conversation without fear of falling into some crevasse of bubbling invectives that have just opened up.

The tragedy is that these tribal hurrahs might prove as phony as the much-maligned product SPAM when it first appeared as a poor replacement for meat, and later (in a different usage when meaning a piece of junk email) as an even worse replacement for a friend's handwritten letter. If loyalty is a fleeting and tradable commodity, is it still loyalty? Without the kin skin in the game that existed in our original homes, true loyalty within the hastily gathered "tribes" variously encamped in today's divided world will remain as elusive as it has been since beginning of the human diaspora tens of thousands of years ago. Rather than healing the wounds of alienation, today's tribalism throws salt in them.

That's hardly the type of future anyone would dream of—whether or not it accomplishes karmic rebalancing. Yet that everyone-for-themselves nightmare is exactly what looms as the sun sets on this brief and remarkable interlude known as human history—a continuation of the rat race that devolves into a frenzied effort to assume the fetal position.

So where is this damn transformation we were promised? Where is the apotheosis? Haven't we gone on enough pilgrimages, attended enough Burning Mans, and disturbed enough Amazonians about their strange brews[82] to find whatever it is we were seeking? How is it that, every time we set our compass for home, we

---

82. See https://en.wikipedia.org/wiki/Ayahuasca.

find ourselves back in the wilderness? Seven billion people in the backseat want to know: "Are we there yet?"

We are all just a little bit tired.

Can't we just 3D print the Holy Grail?

In case that allusion isn't familiar to you, the Holy Grail is a legendary motif from the myths that originated in the era of courtly love. The relic was first described by Chrétien de Troyes around 1190 in Perceval, le Conte du Graal, a romantic story famous for being unfinished—as all stories about unrequited love ought to be. The term "holy grail" has since become synonymous with an unattainable goal that is sought for its great significance.

So, is our chase for the Great Society a fool's journey? Should the chase remain an unattained quest? Is the aspiration alone good enough?

Maybe.

If we, the authors, thought so, we wouldn't have bothered putting fingertips to keys. We started you on this particular journey because we believe the idea of a Great Society is not only possible but probable and imminent.

Why? Because the answers are right in front of us.

We're at that "tap your heels together three times" moment when we realize that we have had the power to change our story all along.

The answers are hiding in every great myth and every enduring story. They are hiding in every email we send, in every glance at another human, and in every detail of our everyday lives. They are hiding in worn world history textbooks and in today's endless array of dystopian headlines. If we only were to look.

That's because, seen through a wider lens, the arc of human experience as we know it has been nothing more than an epiphenomenon of our search for something new to replace the inclusive fitness of the tribal era as the rhythm of our shared existence. That's eminently doable.

The elusive chalice not only has been hiding in plain sight—we've been drinking from it.

———————————

Dominoes of history like the Fall of Man and the Fall of Rome are still falling today. We haven't reached, or created, that inflection point of history where we finally bring the inclusive ethos of the kin village to the global village. That inflection point—which we would assign as the year zero—remains on the far horizon. Thus we have before us an opportunity, and an obligation, of epic proportions.

PART III

Race to the Top

CHAPTER NINE

Revolution of the Social Contract

Before the time of written words, oral stories were like people: older versions died, and evolved versions that suited the changing contexts emerged.

All that changed with the invention of writing.

Written stories could outlive their storytellers and compete with descendants' stories. The Gutenberg press accelerated the replication of written stories and enabled the masses to access a growing diversity of stories and formulate their own views.

It was in this setting that a particular book collector in Kraków used the power of books to challenge one of the great ancient stories: that we (planet earth) are the center of the universe.

Nicolaus Copernicus amassed a sizable library of astronomy books during the late 15th century, and in 1549 he published his own synthesis of the newly unleashed information, On the Revolutions of Heavenly Spheres. In his book, Copernicus transformed a convoluted, geocentric model of planetary motion into the elegant heliocentric model that we have today. All prior stories had us as the center of existence, thus the notion that our lives were orbiting around a body other than our own planet was nothing short of earth shattering.

Indeed, the conceptual reframing of existing, seemingly esoteric data to explain the revolution of celestial bodies was so radical that the word revolution became synonymous with the now-familiar notion of overthrowing an established system. Dominoes have been falling ever since: the French Revolution, the American Revolution, the Internet Revolution, the Blockchain Revolution, and the Artificial Intelligence Revolution.

Today, we are a quarter century into the Internet Revolution. As profound as the impact of Gutenberg's printing press was on the spread of ideas that helped spark the Renaissance, it pales in comparison to the liberation of knowledge achieved through the Internet. This begs the following question: what will be the Copernican Revolution of our time?

On the one hand, looking to the Copernican Revolution for inspiration may feel like a stale analogy that we've moved far beyond; our understanding of astronomy and physics is—with due apology—light years ahead of where we were in the middle of the last millennium.

On the other hand, the Copernican Revolution might just be the perfect analogy for the revolution of our social contract with each other. The social version of the Copernican Revolution could do to egocentrism what the astronomical version did to its anagramic cousin, geocentrism: make someone else the central star of our lives.

Past efforts suggest that trying to get people to understand that we might not be the center of the universe is non-trivial. Self-centrism has an innate appeal that other-centrism can only envy. The battle between them is akin to Goliath versus David, but without a slingshot.

Those who have put their skin in the game to try to get people to accept the idea of putting others at the center of life have paid a large price. Jesus gave up his life. Copernicus feared the potential reaction to his book, and his own reaction upon being presented the first printing was to drop dead.[83] Galileo Galilei, found guilty of heresy for carrying on the Copernican view, was sentenced to indefinite confinement and forced to read seven penitential psalms a week. In the spirit of

83. Bell, E. T. (1992/1940). *The development of mathematics*. New York: Dover.

kin skin in the game, his daughter Maria Celeste relieved him of that punishment by securing ecclesiastical permission to take it upon herself.[84]

When defending an underdog position in a memetic parallax, Galileo's fate exemplifies the perils of resistance against self-dealing, self-expanding beasts (as a reminder from Part II, these metaphorical beasts refer to socio-political-economic institutions that self-expand through extractive capitalism, such as the healthcare system, Big Food, and fake news).[85] The years leading up to his trial were characterized by the typical escalation of mob mentality, unnecessary theater, and polarization of camps. If anything, opposition to heliocentrism became entrenched. It wasn't until after Isaac Newton published Principia in 1687—nearly half a century after Galileo's death—that the heliocentric view became generally accepted.[86]

Is there another way for an underdog to win without throwing stones, fighting through the resistance, and alienating—or being alienated by—the very opponent they are trying to persuade?

Aikido, the Art of Peace, is a martial art form known for using the opponent's own force against them.[87] One common maneuver is to use an opponent's momentum to throw them to the mat. Harnessing the adversary's energy enables the actor to fell much larger opponents.

Revolutionizing our social contract will require a fundamental shift in our culture. Self-dealing has been the prevailing human behavior for so long, and been so well rewarded, that its hold on culture is pervasive. Self-expanding beasts are towering over society everywhere on the horizon.

So what's the big idea here? Slay these self-expanding beasts one by one? That's not a sensible approach, for several reasons. First, it would be futile, as the

84. Shea, W. (2006). *The Galileo affair*. Unpublished work, Grupo de Investigación sobre Ciencia, Razón y Fe.
85. His opponents used the absence of Stellar Parallax as proof against heliocentrism.
86. Kobe, D. H. (1998). Copernicus and Martin Luther: An encounter between science and religion. *American Journal of Physics, 66*, 190.
87. See https://en.wikipedia.org/wiki/Aikido.

system would self-select other beasts to arise in their place, just like a bad Whack-a-Zombie apocalypse. Second, the beasts are comprised of the exact community of people we are trying to protect. Third, as discussed above, we might be the beast, not the hero.

A better approach may be to recognize that the beasts are second-order symptoms. Trying to address the second-order symptom before solving the first-order problem will lead to third-order derivative issues.

The first order of business, then, is to create a system of inclusive stakeholding to replace inclusive fitness as the fundamental social contract of humanity.

We are optimistic about this.

We are optimistic because there are a lot of tools at our collective disposal. We are not limited to rewriting fairy tales, such as the Hero's Journey. For a world that has remained flat-footed on innovations for incentives, there has never been a better environment and a greater need to offer radical solutions. In the following chapters, we chart a path to develop these solutions based on cultural, biological, and technological tools that are already available:

Shifting cultural norms—cultural reprogramming—from egocentrism to interdependence through linguistic invention: the creation and propagation of new words and cultural concepts

Cultural reprogramming through expanding the field of psychology from the current first-person perspective to include second- and third-person perspectives

Cultural reprogramming through a channel of trust: packaging messages in music subverts the inherent neural reflex that detects whether the message is coming from someone familiar (such as kin)

Redesigning the fundamental social contract to enable the creation of Interdependent Capitalism through Inclusive Stakeholding—or Interdependent Stakeholding

We discuss how Blockchain smart contracts could be designed to reshape incentives across society to create better alignment, thus forming the basis for a new type of social contract. And, finally, we describe an incentive prize that we, the Yun family, established in the fall of 2018 that is designed to encourage people imagine better system of incentives.

Throughout these chapters, we also discuss how to use existing forces—that is, to apply the Aikido principle—to power the tools, rather than fighting against the forces that established the current conditions. In other words, we are optimistic that the existing forces driving the "self" culture can be redirected to a self-driving revolution against the culture of self-centeredness.[88] That is, to use everything the beast is good at for the greater good and take advantage of the beast's innate instinct to take advantage.

In the ancient tradition of the ouroboros, let the snake eat itself.[89]

---

88. The key components of self-driving revolutions are (1) feed the beast its own tail, i.e., redirect the natural forces of systems to self-correct the dysfunctions; (2) write the decentralization of power into the movement's self-replicating code, i.e., giving others the stage, credit, resources, and voice.
89. See https://en.wikipedia.org/wiki/Ouroboros.

CHAPTER TEN

Independence and Interdependence

Independence Day in the United States is a federal holiday celebrating the adoption of the Declaration of Independence on July 4, 1776 against the British Crown. The American Revolution was sparked in part by the ideal of individual rights espoused by liberal thinkers such as John Locke, Jean-Jacques Rousseau, and Charles-Louis de Secondat, Baron de La Brède et de Montesquieu. The holiday is commonly associated with fireworks and political speeches that commemorate the history, government, and traditions of the United States.

The Declaration of Independence was no doubt a monumental event, but how do we reconcile the celebration of independence with the reality that, a quarter millennium later, Britain is now a close ally in the emerging global village? Does it make sense to keep throwing parades about signing divorce papers when we are, in fact, living together again?

Indeed, all nations today are living together in a highly interconnected world. Our fates are intertwined, as individuals and nations, like never before. From ecological impact to interdigitated financial systems, we all have a collective interest in managing the risks and opportunities across the planet.

Here are some fundamental questions. Are we going to use the connectivity to scale our localized self-dealing, extractive behaviors to the global level? Are we going to stand by and watch digital versions of imperialism, colonialism, and crusades take hold at the expense of the many? Are we going to keeping feeding the self-expanding beasts in their race to the middle? Or are we going to use the global connectivity to spread the very best of our human values? Whatever we do, the stakes have never been higher.

Our mind's tendency to espouse separatism—the way we did with the separation of good and evil in Eden, the way we did with Beowulf and Grendel, the way we have done in every story we've told ourselves—is not only illusory but dangerous. It's the greatest existential threat to our future.

On the other hand, embracing interdependence may be our most significant existential hope. Imagine a global holiday called Interdependence Day.

CHAPTER ELEVEN

Psychology 2.0

Holidays are important cultural rituals. They connect us to deeper tribal traditions related to birth, death, harvest, atonement, sacrifice, love, and the passage of time. Who among us remembers that the root meaning of the word holiday is "holy day"? Today in the West, the hallmark of a holiday is more often than not a material transaction like a Hallmark card—another example of an ancient virtue commodified by the race to the bottom line. If we are to promote the notion of celebrating our interdependence, it will take more than exchanging cardboard reminders once a year that all but report our negligence the other 364 days.

Is there a way to turn the appreciation of our interdependence into an everyday cultural norm? We absolutely think so, and we believe we can do so using tools already available to us.

First, we envision leveraging the growing public interest in the field of psychology. Once the domain of the elite or the fringe, today even mainstream folks are taking an interest in understanding habits of the mind and how they can help shape behaviors. But the field of psychology itself is due for an update.

For starters, we need to get out of our own heads.

In Part II, we described the emergence of first-person psychology led by Freud and Maslow—the obsession with selfhood—as the latest symptom of solitarity's triumph over solidarity. The cultural reprogramming of our social contract, then, begins with extending the field of psychology from the first-person perspective to one that also includes second- and third-person perspectives.

Life is an intensely personal, and most often self-centered, experience. Psychology 2.0 will be about including the interests of someone else in that experience. To give you a sense of our blind spots, the basic four-quadrant chart below shows how Person A reacts to the experience of Person B—another human being:

	PERSON B IS SUCCESSFUL	PERSON B IS SUFFERING
If Person A's response to B's state is happiness, then it is called:	?	schadenfreude
If Person A's response to B's state is sadness, then it is called:	freudenschade (envy)	compassion

Schadenfreude and freudenschade[90] (envy) are psychological expressions of the zero-sum-game mentality we've all witnessed. The former is a happy feeling caused by another's misfortune. The latter is a sad feeling caused by another's success.

Meanwhile, compassion is the sadness we feel for the suffering of another person.

What, then, is the term for a person experiencing happiness for the success of another person?

Exactly.

If you were to ask this of a room containing one hundred people, it would be a small miracle if even one person called out the word compersion. A word for the feeling is elusive in other cultures as well and the concept has remained unnamed in many languages. Most Buddhists, for example, are unfamiliar with the word mudita, which describes the Buddhist concept of vicarious joy.

---

90.   See https://www.recruiter.com/i/which-is-worse-professional-schadenfreude-or-freudenschade/; https://web.archive.org/web/20080513182307/http://daily.stanford.edu/article/2006/4/28/freuden-schade.

In other words, one of the four most basic psychological experiences we have in the context of a second person is still awaiting its recognition in many vocabularies. That is a stunning omission.

And yet, compersion is a universal experience in one particular context: parents' experience of their children. Parents experience a quiet (and sometimes not so quiet) joy when their child succeeds. Evolution selected our nature to nurture and encoded this emotional response as a reward reflex to promote inclusive fitness. However, high-alignment relationships such as family are less common in today's low-alignment world.

Compersion and compassion are the inherent psychological dynamics when there is high alignment. Is there a way to make these experiences and emotions far more common than freudenschade and schadenfreude in today's global society? Compassion is a well-known and widely embraced emotion that is often preached and practiced. Its prevalence is related to the word's frequent appearance in popular culture. Imagine if we could promote the word compersion to that level of familiarity and high regard.

That would make us happy.

Compassion and compersion are considered precursor concepts to empathy and are analogous to many notions that appear in all cultures, including the Golden Rule: "Do upon others as you would want done upon you."[91] The Golden Rule can be thought of as a social codification of inclusive fitness: a mother's kind act toward her child is partially a kind act to herself, given her 50 percent vested interest in the child's genes.

What's lacking from that framing is the experience from the perspective of the recipient, the second- or third-person perspective. In Part II we mentioned that no word exists to denote the feeling of "seeking empathy"—a fundamental human

---

91. See https://en.wikipedia.org/wiki/Golden_Rule.

experience. Many other fundamental experiences of second-person psychology also have not been named.

Here are some examples. We know a lot about envy, but we don't know much about the psychology of "wanting to be envied." So much of human pursuit today, including posting on social media, reflects the desire to produce a feeling of envy in others—the feeling of "wanting to be popular." Yet we don't have a word for the feeling.

Similarly, no English word precisely captures the traits of "seeking compassion," "seeking to be understood," "seeking validation," or "seeking to be the object of curiosity." These are definitional phrases awaiting the invention of precise neologisms. The closest approximation of a word that captures the general feelings of seeking empathy, compassion, understanding, curiosity or validation is "needy," a pejorative term that doesn't do justice to these concepts.

Systems psychology—psychology 2.0 or inclusive psychology—remains hugely underdeveloped.[92] As Freud and subsequent psychologists did for psychology 1.0, we can kickstart inclusive psychology by starting to name the basic second- and third-person psychological phenomena described above.

Assigning neologisms to phenomena has a way of creating consciousness. Collective consciousness is culture. So, cultural shift is possible by creating a lexicon that makes us more conscious and mindful of the experience of others. Creating a new vocabulary for inclusive psychology can promote awareness of others in our lives, just as the creation of terms such as "self-help," "self-advocacy," and "self-love" did to form the consciousness of the self movement.

In some cases, redefining familiar words in new ways can help create a new consciousness. Too many so-called leaders (think of influencers) of today try to amass followers. Imagine instead a world in which the definition of leadership is "to steward the leadership potential of others." That ethos was genetically codified in the kin tribe of yore, but it has all but disappeared in modern low-align-

---

92. See http://psycnet.apa.org/record/1998-12339-008.

ment communities and institutions, except in some cases in the way parents raise their kids in nuclear families.

As mentioned in Part II, the most important aspect of these concepts is not the concepts themselves but how they are used. Machine learning algorithms can be trained to be empathetic to human users—that is, to understand what a person is experiencing—and then use that information to exploit humans instead of serving them. These tools are not inherently the issue; the intentions of the humans behind them are.

In this regard, syntax or grammar can be used in profoundly new ways to promote greater awareness of our responsibility to others instead of focusing on others' responsibility to us (i.e., our entitlements).

Here's an example. Think about world issues and find a way to turn a "they statement" into an "I statement." This can turn a depressing third-person situation and into a personal responsibility and action item. For example, "California is not doing enough to keep the highways clean" can be restated as "I need to adopt my neighborhood highway so I can keep it clean." The reverse process is cool too. When something good happens, turn an "I statement" into a "you statement": "I scored the game winning goal" becomes "Your pass led to the game winning goal." These processes help us look for people to appreciate and we can begin to include others in our story.

Words have the power to shape our culture, and we have the power to create new words—and create new uses of existing words—that can help shift our psychological frame from individuality to interdependence.

When it comes to psychology, it's not just me, it's also you.

Speaking of leaders, in his inaugural address, President John F. Kennedy beseeched his countrymen, "Ask not what your country can do for you; ask what you can do for your country." Such antimetaboles can be used as a tool to reprogram the public to become more aware of a contrarian notion. It was thus, in the throes of the Cold War and another conflict that was heating up, that Kennedy launched the Peace Corps.

We might have preferred a version of that statement that better reflects the competing dualities of a memetic parallax—that we are the hero and the beast—by inserting the words "only" and "also": "Ask not only what your country can do for you; ask also what you can do for your country."

But that's being a bit nitpicky, like pointing out that the heliocentric model is also off target, given the reality that the sun and the earth revolve around the center of gravities of "each other."[93] Or like pointing out that the founder of the Peace Corps also took the world to the brink of a nuclear war.[94]

For the moment, anyone who can point the world to a contrarian truth, as Kennedy did with his antimetabole, is at least helping split a consensus mob into a memetic parallax so that our responsibilities to others become more apparent. That alone is one small step for mankind. It would be a giant leap to recognize duality as the enduring truth.

———————

Let's get back on a higher plane.

Creating a new vocabulary and cultural programming through psychology 2.0 is one thing; it's another thing entirely to drive their adoption. Psychology 1.0 taught us that the human brain is prone to confirmation bias: the tendency to find things that confirm our existing beliefs. Unfamiliar concepts tend to elicit suspicion and skepticism. How do we break through such psychological barriers to adoption?

Rather than trying to convey messages in a way that goes unheard, in the next chapter we will discuss a method that has been proven to work in reshaping minds and hearts—a method that everyone is intimately familiar with already: music.

---

93. And in relationship to the center of gravity of all other heavenly bodies.
94. See https://en.wikipedia.org/wiki/Cuban_Missile_Crisis.

CHAPTER TWELVE

Mother's Voice

Fifty years ago, Jeremy's grandfather Sung Hee Yun appeared on Walter Cronkite's national TV program due to his work of inserting public education into pop songs—work that later landed him a career at the World Bank, where he collaborated with musicians around the globe to create positive social change. His work proved what we already know in our hearts—that music can change the world.

A song is among the oldest forms of communications in nature—older than human language and even older than humans. The role of song in social evolution cannot be overestimated.

Music's ongoing role in culture today also cannot be overestimated. We are more connected to the music of our artists than ever before. But something doesn't quite feel right. Music today feels commodified. Given the population's increasing interconnectedness without kin skin in the game, the music industry is incentivized to self-deal and profit at the audience's expense. The relationship between artists and fans is now more like the Supertramp song "Goodbye Stranger" than the Stephen Stills' song "Love the One You're With."

The music industry has become another victim of the race to the bottom—another self-expanding beast. The music "ecosystem" selects for songs that compete for audience attention with escalating titillations. One hundred years ago, the words used most often in the lyrics of popular songs were gems, rag, home, land, and old. The words used most often in popular songs today are we, yeah, hell, fuck, and die.[95] Today's commodified songs, produced to maximize profit, put money in the hands of producers who repeat the cycle.

95. See http://www.prooffreader.com/2014/12/most-decade-specific-words-in-billboard.html.

The point isn't to put the genie—the power of music—back in the bottle. That would be futile anyway. The point is to leverage that power for good, as per the Aikido principle. And there's an even bigger point. The change that matters most is changing who we serve: ourselves or others. That begs the following question: are we going to use our connecting powers to spread hate and fear, or to spread the very best of our human values?

That's a question for the ages.

––––––––––––––––––––

What makes music so potent in its capacity for cultural reprogramming?

Jeremy's grandfather taught us that, when it comes to spreading human values, it's not just the message that matters but also how it's delivered. Neuroscience has shown that people respond to the same message differently depending on the context: who said it, the tone of voice, and so on.

Here's an example. We know that words heard by the right ear go to the left hemisphere of the brain, and words heard by the left ear go to the right side. The left hemisphere processes language and is more predisposed to positive impressions. Normally, this asymmetry doesn't make a difference because we hear with both ears. However, when whispering into one ear or hearing through headsets and earpieces, choosing the left or right ear could make a difference. A recent study showed that making a request into the right ear got far more positive responses than making the same request into the left ear. Think about that when you are about to whisper sweet nothings into someone's ear.

Humor and music also allow an audience to engage with a message through different pathways in the brain than do words alone. Notably, words packaged in the delivery vehicle of familiar music is a particularly effective way to bypass mental defenses against messages. Familiar music activates the same neural (emotional, primal) reward reflex as when a baby hears a mom's voice, a critical source of emotional comfort and social learning.

Why does mimicking the mother's voice reflex work in conveying a message? What is the original purpose of the mother's voice reflex in nature?

Fake news is as old as biology. As mentioned earlier, the most important thing about a message is who gives it to you. Mom may not know best, but she cares about you most by virtue of Hamilton's rule. That's why evolution wired us to trust our mother's voice more than any other voice. If we did nothing but listen to our mom over everyone else who might be trying to exploit us, it would on average lead to a good outcome. Our mom's version of how to live life is most valuable for us, not because she has the best information but because she cares about us (on average) more than anyone else does. As the saying goes, "Life doesn't come with a manual. It comes with a mom." That's kin skin in the game at its zenith.

So why does familiar music trigger this reflex? In the primordial evolutionary epoch before words, there was song. From a teleological perspective, hearing a familiar song may have meant you were hearing from someone who has been around you for a while: your family.

Indeed, the words familiar and family come from the same Latin root, familia, which connotes a domestic group that includes cousins, aunts, and uncles across multiple generations—in other words, a kin tribe. So, a familiar song was a sign of the presence of someone who had your best interests at heart.

When nature selected songs as a mechanism for kin signaling, it never anticipated an evolutionary future in which recorded music could repeat the same song. Songs once served as a unique acoustic fingerprint of a family member; now they are industrially replicated to draw your affection and attention.

On the one hand, this sounds depressing. On the other hand, it bodes well.

Familiar music's ability to trigger the same neural reward reflex as hearing one's mother's voice can be used reshape culture in a positive direction. The same reflexes the music industry uses to extract profits from the public can be repurposed to serve the public instead.

Other art forms can help do this too, but music has unique powers. People tend to sing along to songs they hear, which reinforces messages, and people like to sing together, which spreads messages. Think about that.

The troubadours showed the world that music could reshape the cultures of love, heroism, and valor, even during a time of social and monastic oppression. Jeremy's grandfather showed it too, through his work.

In keeping with the Aikido principle, global connectivity—the very force that is challenging human values—can spread the very best of our human values through music.

We've covered a lot of ground about cultural reprogramming. We talked about reshaping social norms through cultural rituals, language, psychology, and art forms. At the end of the day, however, our intuition tells us that their effectiveness will be limited. They will be limited for the same reason commandments, decrees, memes, laws, and stories go only so far in reshaping social norms.

No doubt some people will be moved to rethink their approach to life and abide by new norms. For the vast majority, however, the temptations of self-interest will remain too powerful to override. We need something more powerful than counterculture concepts.

We will need to harness self-interest itself to fuel the cultural reprogramming we have provided examples of in Part III.

We will give this notion a name: Interdependent Capitalism.

CHAPTER THIRTEEN

Interdependent Capitalism

"Man is born free, and everywhere he is in chains." That's the opening sentence of Jean-Jacques Rousseau's The Social Contract. Written in 1762, Rousseau defines man's natural state as being free and happy, and man's loss of autonomy in the modern world as being the root of alienation, injustice, unhappiness, abuse, and war.

We make a different claim.

We claim that man's natural state is interdependence and that, without sufficient mutual vested interest to reflect that interdependence, man's pursuit of autonomy and enlightened self-interest has also been a source of alienation, injustice, unhappiness, abuse, and war.

Is there a way to reconcile these seemingly conflicting philosophies? Absolutely.

The common ground is this. Independence without mutual vested interest can promote the extractive behaviors and abuses we fear. Interdependence without mutual vested interest can also promote the kinds of extractive behaviors and abuses that Rousseau feared. Thus the debate ought not to be about the merits of independence versus interdependence. It ought to be about the lack of mutual vested interest.

Indeed, if mutually vested interest is properly designed as the social contract in an interdependent network, man's innate tendency to pursue self-interest can be harnessed to work for mutual benefit rather than extraction. That is, social algorithms for inclusive stakeholding can be designed to mimic the bioalgorithms of inclusive fitness.[96] Goal congruence increases with the degree of mutually vested interest.[97]

Can we tie the success of teachers to that of their pupils? Can we tie the success of health insurance, food, and media companies—and every industry—to that of their customers as well as the public interest? Can we tie the success of elected officials to that of their constituents? Can we find ways to include the environment, future generations, and others without a voice as stakeholders? Can we redesign physical and online communities around the right mix of diversity and common interests the way kin tribes once did?

We believe that the recent emergence of Blockchain and related technologies represents an unprecedented platform to instantiate this vision: to create vested interest among interdependent stakeholders, inclusively defined, the way inclusive fitness did for kin tribes[98] It would be akin to taking the notion of employee stock options common in Silicon Valley companies and extending it to users, consumers, and other stakeholders.[99]

Establishing goal congruence through vested interest among stakeholders in such a way would fundamentally transform every dimension of society.

We hope that, by shedding light on the origins of our modern self-dealing behavior, people can take more enlightened positions about the way we treat each other.

96. Inclusive stakeholding is the notion that all potential stakeholders of an institution are given appropriate amounts of skin in the game.
97. For example, if a social media company, advertisers, and users co-owned stakes in each other's success, the incentives for extractive behavior would be proportionally reduced. They would have a higher degree of goal congruence than if they didn't have such mutually vested interest.
98. To date, however, some Blockchain initiatives have been characterized by the same self-dealing behaviors of traditional institutions. In fact, generally speaking, applying the powers of technologies to the same human foibles only amplifies the abuses. Other recent examples of this trend include social media companies, artificial intelligence, and robots. On the other hand, these risks could be turned into assets if we created a model of vested interest in the success of others. Rather than developing policies to regulate these runaway institutions, we can design "policies" that promote desired social behaviors within technology protocols (e.g., smart contracts).
99. Blockchain and token economic models are able to supersede the traditional theory of the firm and blur the lines between shareholder, consumer, and other stakeholders in the broader community.

It is our nature to nurture those in whom we have a vested stake. But we can do better. We don't have to rely on nature or our upbringing (nurture) to govern our decisions and actions. We also can act with personal agency. We can choose to do the right thing for others, simply as a matter of personal choice. Reprogramming culture is part of that.

However, we may not be able to count on personal agency to override people's hardwired tendency to self-deal; we believe the key will be in creating new social contracts that give people vested interest in the success of others.

To be clear, however, there is no such thing as a perfect system of incentives. Even kin tribes undergo rapid dilution of alignment as lineages arborize. It is also perfectly common for even close families to become estranged and scatter. Either way, every house becomes divided over the generations, dispersing into self-replicating units of new hives. Imprinting on siblings promotes dispersion, outbreeding, and diversity among progeny while deleterious homozygous diseases punish inbreeding. Dispersion, in short, is a feature of social evolution and not a bug. The rapid dilution of shared genetic interest foments greater degrees of competition between groups as the generations unfold, but within each new group, collaboration is the rule.

It seems that some balance of competing interests and alignment of interests within social groups maximizes evolutionary fitness across spatial and temporal fractals. In other words, the diversity of competing interests, like alignment of interest, is a feature—and not necessarily a bug—of complex social systems. Speciation, population diasporas, and Blockchain forks result from, and contribute to, the emergence of complex ecosystems featuring a mix of diversity, competition, and collaboration.

There is also no such thing as the "right" mix of these features for any particular ecosystem, as a system will adapt as necessary over time. However, that adaptation won't happen soon enough for humans living today. Furthermore, ignoring the cancer of perverse incentives will only lead to a metastasis of self-dealing behaviors.[100]

We need solutions today. Rather than being prescriptive, however, we believe that in the proper context solutions can be produced from the collective power of the community by the very elements that power evolution: competition and coopetition.

In that spirit, our family launched an impact initiative in 2018 aimed at nurturing innovations, including Blockchain, that help reimagine our institutions based on the concept of Inclusive Stakeholding. We believe in the bottom-up philosophy that each community—when properly incentivized to do so—is in the best position to create incentive structures that serve the greatest good.

Thus, as part of our initiative on Inclusive Stakeholding, we have launched an incentive prize for incentives to develop a new model called Interdependent Capitalism (a.k.a. Interdependent Stakeholding).[101] Competition is a natural force of social systems, and we are leveraging this force to nurture the best ideas for social innovation on incentives.

Buckminster Fuller said, "You never change things by fighting the existing reality. To change something, build a new model that makes the existing model obsolete."

We will all be aligned with the success of our ideas. Whereas misalignment with competition is a race to the bottom, alignment with competition is a race to the top—another example of the Aikido principle. If we succeed, our transformative journey from the kin tribe to the connected global village—a return home from the diaspora in the Joseph Campbell sense—will be complete.

Let's write the story of how we will find our way back home.

---

100. Perhaps inserting vested interest into the genetic code of rogue cancer cells could help the "beast" domesticate itself back to being a constructive member of the interdependent system called the body.
101. See https://www.prnewswire.com/news-releases/yun-family-foundation-sponsors-an-incentive-prize-on-incentives----a-10-000-research-paper-prize-on-the-research-topic-inclusive-stakeholding-reimagining-incentives-to-promote-the-greater-good-in-the-new-journal-frontiers-in--300768275.html.

CHAPTER FOURTEEN

Welcome Home

We hope by now that you have a new view of the arc of human history. Evolution selected our innate social instincts, including altruistic behaviors, to align with kin-based social systems. For the longest time, before the era of social mobility, energy-powered dispersion, and diaspora-driven collisions between tribes, it probably was difficult for early humans to avoid living in kin tribes. The fitness value of kin-based living was too high, as was the cost of avoiding it. That was our Eden—our social nirvana of time immemorial.

In that cradle of human social evolution, since our instinctive social behaviors unfolded to maximize fitness, there was less need for higher-order cognitive processing. Indeed, higher-order cognition that overrides innate instincts might even have interfered with fitness maximization. It might be no accident, then, that human societies during the kin tribe era left us no record. Perhaps life for them just was.

Somewhere along the way, we humans became seduced by knowledge, including the knowledge of how to harness energy and make tools. That knowledge uprooted humans from our kin tribes. As lineages arborized, kinship thinned. The hive became a house divided. Descendants battled and were banished to a life of wandering. The diaspora began, fueled by a feed-forward accrual of knowledge and journeys. The dispersion and diaspora hit their planetary limits and the low-aligned lineages merged and remixed.

The journey has been mostly good, but in some ways not so good. The human experience over the past ten thousand years has brought an ever-increasing awareness of the existence of good and bad, expressed through the service or disservice of others, either according to, or in spite of, Hamilton's rule. The battle between these forces has been as dramatic as the prehistoric kin tribe era was (from our vantage point) undramatic. Civilizations began to rise and fall. Strange things started to happen regularly. It began to be worthwhile to observe, contemplate, and act in profoundly new ways.

But by and large, we've had to learn by trial and error. Ideas that seemed good to the parade of conquerors, revolutionaries, and social reformers that have disproportionately shaped our collective history frequently delivered disappointing—if not downright destructive—results. Yet we were never quite sure why they didn't work. Even though we have made great progress in improving our material existence and extending our lifespans—improvements that continue—the rising tide that has buoyed us materially has unmoored us spiritually. Way too many parts of the human experience feel soulless. For the vast majority of people alive today, the price of progress has been a loss of the deep kin identities that were the anchors of human identity for most of the history of our species. We have argued in this book that this cost has been significant—and, even more to the point, one we have not even begun to seriously recognize or address.

We are genetically wired for the kin tribe but we no longer live as such. That's a first-order problem that continues to spawn second-, third-, and fourth-order issues in a degenerating cascade. It's time to get back to the origin.

It's time to restart at year zero.[102]

––––––––––––––

Just as Caesar had no idea that future historians would count the calendar years of his reign in a backwards regression to zero, just as every person basking in the sunlight a thousand years ago was unaware that Petrarch would retroactively label their era the Dark Ages, and just as everyone once thought the earth was bigger

102. Let's close a loop. About a thousand years ago in the East, the Yun family kin tribe was born. About a thousand years ago in the West, an event that had occurred two thousand years before was assigned the year zero. For a variety of historical reasons, in the retrofitted version of events recorded on the Gregorian calendar, year zero does not exist between 1 BCE and 1 CE. The year zero remains unassigned. With the advent of an entirely new form of social order that we call interdependent stakeholding, we are at the dawn of a new era, a transformative inflection point that we can call year zero. With all of the progress we have made as a civilization, we've come full circle back to 0. That's where we are, right now.

than the sun, we today are blind to the possibility that our journey forward has been a journey homeward.

We left our kin village. We envisioned our role as the hero that would slay the beast. We instead got cast in the role of the villain by an unconditionally loving hero. It turned out that these stock archetypes are the farthest things from the truth. There never was a beast to slay or a hero to worship. The same actor has been behind all the roles. Us.

To be clear, the purpose of this book is not to swing the pendulum of human endeavor from self-dealing to self-sacrifice. The truth of human nature lies more in the deep and enduring tension that exists between these extremes than in the extremes themselves.

The story we are telling is decidedly less dramatic than either a destiny of unavoidable and perpetual self-dealing or a resurrection of centuries-old, and centuries-failed, calls for constant universal martyrdom. Our story is that our lives—all of our lives—are best served by encompassing some mix of both modes of living. Enlightened self-interest as a social code works best when we also have a vested interest in each other's lives.

Most importantly, going forward we have the opportunity to reinvent our institutions based on inclusive stakeholding, goal congruence, and vested interest in the success of others—attributes that were inherent in the inclusive fitness of our prehistoric social systems.

We now are stewarding each other's journey homeward. We return not as heroes and nor as the prodigal sons and daughters, but as both. The two sets of footprints we left in the wilderness are now one set, not because one is carrying the other but because as we head home we are whole again.

Instead of a world in which history is written by the victors, imagine a world in which history is made by helping others win.

Epilogue

The tree of life is a mythological archetype that appears throughout the world's religious and philosophical traditions.[103] A branching tree is also employed as a metaphor for evolutionary speciation, Blockchain forks, and many other systems that feature ramifications.

What is a branch point in a tree? Analogous to memetic parallax, a branch point is where ramification—a division—occurs (e.g., the duality of good and evil in the tree of knowledge in Genesis). In a tree, a common central trunk bifurcates into separate limbs, which bifurcate into branches. The process repeats iteratively until the tips of the leaves.[104] Fractal recursion is evident.

The tree of life can also serve as a metaphor for the diaspora of a kin hive over generations. From a central shared trunk, kin lineage iteratively bifurcates in repeating patterns over time. The further downstream from the central trunk, the more distant the cousins.[105] The processes at each branch point share common features, fractally speaking, just like the hive units of successive generations.

---

103. See https://en.wikipedia.org/wiki/Tree_of_life.

104. Apoptosis or programmed death was discovered in the abscission of leaves. The leaves become part of the biological compost in the vicinity of its own roots, contributing substrate that is recycled for the renewal of life in the general direction of evolutionary progress. One can think about the phenoptosis (programmed aging of humans) the same way. Bodies die, and the components are recycled in the vicinity of the tribe, awaiting to be repurposed for evolutionary progress.

105. If you want to blow your mind, here is an upside-down way to think about the tree of life:
It took 2 parents to make you.
It took 4 grandparents to lead to you.
It took 8 great-grandparents to lead to you.
It took 1000 people 10 generations ago to lead to you.
It took a million people 20 generations ago to lead to you.
From then until now, 2 million people participated in the making of you.
From then until now, 1 million love stories led to the making of you.
That's 1 million couples who chose each other above all others.
That's 1 million love stories in just the last 400 years.
That's 1 million mothers who loved a child.

Conversely, can the diaspora of a kin hive over the generations also serve as a metaphor for the tree? Is a genomic diaspora observable in the ramification of branches within a single tree the way kin genomics ramify? As might have been predicted, based on this thinking, leaf genome sequences on an individual tree were not found to be identical; they varied systematically as a gradient from the bottom to the top of the tree.[106] Thus the genetic variance among branches increases along with the degree of ramification. Each tree exhibits microchimerism.

Though rare, microchimerism is also observed in animals, including humans.[107] We are built through iterations of cell divisions among lineages, starting with the embryo. As genomic tests advance, perhaps we will learn that microchimerism is more common in animals than is observable today. Or, we might learn that genomic ramification—the decline of genetic alignment and the loss of vested interest in the success of other cells—is too problematic for animals to maintain as a whole so that genetic variance is policed out of the body by the immune system. We might find that, as a society of cells, all non-gonadal cells are 100 percent aligned genomically, like a perfectly aligned hive.

This lower tolerance of the genetic diaspora of cell lineages in animals than in trees may relate to the degree of interdependence. If the limbs of a tree are seen as a collection of conjoined cousins, when one cousin dies the remaining branches not only survive, they thrive.[108] The greater tolerance of genetic variance in trees versus animals is evident in the greater ease of grafting transplants. Whereas human cousin groups can tolerate even greater genomic diversity than a tree—their bodies and their fate are not intertwined—when one-half of conjoined humans dies, the whole typically dies.[109] It would seem likely that microchime-

---

106. See https://www.ncbi.nlm.nih.gov/pmc/articles/PMC3937000/.
107. See https://www.ncbi.nlm.nih.gov/pubmed/17917028; http://citeseerx.ist.psu.edu/viewdoc/download?doi=10.1.1.149.9001&rep=rep1&type=pdf.
108. The fate of conjoined humans is similar to when a common trunk of two limbs of a tree dies: the whole unit perishes.
109. That said, there may be more contagious signaling across non-conjoined humans than we realize. Are there senescence pheromones among humans, like the coordinated contagion of senescence through ethylene among leaves in a forest? Here's a related question: Why did nature select for conscious signaling in some cases (spoken word) versus subconscious signaling in other cases (pheromones)? Perhaps there is

rism is less frequent in animals than in trees, and less frequent in trees than in a kin hive as a superorganism.

A human cancer cell, then, is a division gone rogue. Perhaps the immune system clears most cells that have gone rogue, but it is not always successful. Furthermore, a cancer cell can subvert existing host pathways and hijack them to self-deal at the expense of the host. The cancer becomes a self-expanding beast that feeds on the host—a former community member that grows by feeding off the community. The parallels to institutions in our society today are self-evident.

The tree of life metaphor can help distill other themes explored in this book. Given the interdependence among dividing limbs, the bifurcations are dehybridizations characterized by some degree of competition, overall goal congruence, and vested interest in each other's success. The distal branches can be thought of as genetically different cousins who compete with each other for resources from the central trunk below; they grow upwards and past each other competing for sunlight from above.

Given their high degree of interdependence by virtue of their shared trunk, the Darwinian competition among even the most distal leaves are as benign as Little League baseball: enough competitive dynamic to help nurture the selection of beneficial traits among the distal leafy cousins but not enough competition to truly hurt each other.[110]

One can think of competition for resources from the trunk as competition for mother's attention. One can think of the vertical competition for sunlight as competition for father's attention.[111] But the competition is subordinate to their shared fate of interdependence. Combined, the high alignment and com-

---

adaptive benefit in the subconscious coordination of group behaviors.

110. Nature exhibits a diversity of approaches in mixing the degree of competition and alignment in hives. A tree's ratio of collaboration and competition and that of a human tribe is different. However, these can be seen as variations on the theme of a parallax of approaches in evolutionary programming among the plant and animal kingdoms.

111. If we continue with the analogy, one implication of the attraction to the sun is that the evolutionary progress of life on earth may not be just a self-referential unfolding or emergence but a bend toward a certain destiny we are being attracted or pulled to. More generally, given the fractal nature of nature and the expression of the universe as the emergence from recursive functions, we might be able to deduce the totality of the universe by looking at the organization and functions of a tree relative to its surroundings.

petition promote growth. Unlike the inevitable race to the bottom line that emerges when competition occurs in a setting of low alignment, competition in the context of high alignment, such as in the tree of life, engenders the race to the top. Literally.

In the beginning there was light. Actually, some of that light existed separately as mass according to E=mc2. That mass caused light to cast a shadow, separating darkness from light. From the heavens had separated the sun, and from the sun had separated the earth.

Let's start over. In the beginning, there was duality.

For everything to be one, there can be no end to the oneness. If there is an end to one, then there are at least two. Thus the concept of a unifying oneness can only exist as an inferential infinite loop. That's probably enough to keep you up for more than one night.

But this we know: what makes night exist is the day. It takes the second one to make the first exist. What if it takes a second to make existence exist? What if one is derived from two? What if everything is derived from two?

Isn't that how babies are made? Everyone is made from the merger of two, and then everyone finds another to merge with, into one, recursively.

Which came first? The chicken and the egg?

Let's do the do-over, again. In the beginning there were two of everything. When there got to be too many of everything and things got complicated, either fire or water wiped the slate clean to start over, restarting with two of everything again. Or so the story goes. The ark is the arc.

Here comes the story, again. In the beginning, there was duality. To be less inaccurate, there is no beginning or end. Duality is. God and the serpent. Good and evil. It is not about the sacrifices or the transgressions described in this book. Or any other book. It is always about both. Neither is the gift nor the curse. The duality—and the lack of resolution, the lack of peace, the lack of consensus, the lack of unanimity, the lack of equality, the lack of melding into the inferential infinite loop of oneness—is the curse and the gift.

That is, the curse of Whack-a-Mole described in this book, the curse of the never-ending series of revolutions concluded by the rise of the same bosses, is also the gift. How could something nefarious, both the transgression itself and its endless recurrence, be one-half of a two-part gift/curse? At the end of the day, aren't some transgression simply a curse and not a gift?

By the subjective standards we've chosen for the sake of existential convenience, that last statement may be true. By objective reality, however, a transgression is a curse and a gift. The rise of predator beasts who feasted on prey led to the rapid co-evolution of both. That era of unimaginable biologic innovation of form and function is called the Cambrian radiation. Our ability to see the hypocrisy of others while being blind to our own is a gift. People aren't good or evil; everyone is good and evil. The curse of human dualities, the conflicts between capitalism versus socialism, the tribal wars, the upheaval of religions versus the secular, the red versus blue states, boy versus girl, is the gift that drives transformation. We didn't just get expelled from Eden; we were birthed. The rain makes the flowers grow.

Aren't we now disagreeing with ourselves? Didn't we spend the entirety of the book opening the wound to heal it? Didn't we begin the story by explaining that we started at home with the kin tribe as a unanimous superorganism, split from each other, went from solidarity to solitarity, got derailed by the dualities to the point of dysfunction, made the clock run down to zero so we can start over again, journey together with our domesticated dualities back to home, so that we could merge all the competing dualities into one aligned superorganism again? Wasn't this treatment of the arc of history just a long-winded way to get from the kin village to the global village? Wasn't this just one big round trip?

Books by their nature can only offer limited vistas. What's outside the vista? If fractal recursion is true, what's inside the book should reveal a glimpse of what's outside the book. What's inside the book, if one were to chart it rather than read it, is a bending descending arc that rises to put us back to sea level by the end. Is what ensues outside the book another scooped U arc? Or will it form an upside-down U? Our vista is limited, but we should be able to use it to surmise the rest.

The form factor of this book is also its own limitation. If there is a prologue, what was before the prologue? If there is an epilogue, what comes after the epilogue? What if we put the prologue after the epilogue and make this into one circular never-ending monologue? Not to worry. There's always the other side of the story. It really is a never-ending dialogue.

The circle is a symbol as well as a reality. The reality is that, if you render a circle into a moving axis, it looks like a sine wave—the path of a serpent, an animal whose path forms the shape of the number 2. If you render the moving circle onto an orthogonal axis, it looks like a spiral.

A circle is the essence of duality. The self-feeding beast turns out to be a self-consuming serpent. That is nothing other than the circle of life itself.

And thus a story begins.

Related Essays

On Math and Language

Many precipitating factors help explain the emergence of advanced symbolic systems, such as language and math, during human evolution. However, the role of the fundamental shift of human relationships—from one predominantly based on kin altruism to one based on reciprocal altruism between counterparties—in the development of advanced symbolic systems cannot be underestimated.

During the kin tribe era, we could generally rely on others acting with our best interests at heart without performing and undue amount of due diligence. Today, reciprocal altruism is the dominant form of human transaction and we now have to count the beans to ascertain if the transactions are fair. Consuming the counterparty risk of strangers is a far cry from suckling the milk of a mother who loved us unconditionally.

Language no doubt increases the evolutionary fitness of social systems based on kin altruism. However, language is even more important for social systems that have to rely predominantly on reciprocal altruism. Counterparty risk is far higher among genetic strangers than genetic relatives. Things and concepts have to be more precisely named, described, and accounted for in the context of negotiating with counterparties who are incentivized to exploit rather than serve each other.

Evolution is an "as is" phenomenon, and teleology as an explanatory style remains controversial. "Why" questions are generally shunned in science as they cannot be empirically validated with experimental tools. Trying to explain the evolutionary emergence of human language is even more problematic, given the paucity of direct evidence. Indeed, the Linguistic Society of Paris's prohibition against debating the topic in 1866 remained influential in suppressing formal discourse on the subject in academia until very recently.[112]

Nonetheless, since the time of Darwin, people have speculated as to why language may have emerged during human evolution. Today, varying hypotheses exist as to where, when, how, and why language may have emerged, but there is scant agreement among them.[113] Furthermore, while many have attempted to link the emergence of language with the emergence of modern human behavior, there is little agreement as to the nature of this association. The full list of hypotheses about the putative link are explored elsewhere.

To that list we would like to add another potential hypothesis. What if the shift from living in kin-based social systems to living in communities of strangers—which lowers genetic alignment and increases counterparty risk—was a forcing function in the acceleration of advanced symbolic systems such as language?

When genetic alignment is higher, the need to negotiate is lower. One can assume that actions within a community are more likely to serve the interests of others and the group. On the other hand, when alignment is low, interactions require a greater degree of negotiation. Subtleties and nuances matter more and the precision that comes with naming things, actions, and abstractions enhances the ability of members in a low-aligned community to negotiate more effectively.

A specific case of this hypothesis as it applies to the advanced symbolic systems is worth further discussion: the emergence of modern numerical systems based on linear scales. In highly aligned social systems, where the conveyance of numerical information is on behalf of a relative rather than against a stranger, representation of quantities can be expressed in a compressive scale where there is high resolution

112. Stam, J. H. (1976). *Inquiries into the origins of language*. New York: Harper and Row, p. 255.
113. Tallerman, M., & Gibson, K. R. (2012). *The Oxford handbook of language evolution*. Oxford, UK: Oxford University Press.

at low numbers and low resolution at high numbers.[114] For instance, as a default, a language might only need to contain the symbols for one, two, several, many, and innumerable.

The benefits of using compressive scales to express quantities are the following. They efficiently represent a wide dynamic range of quantities the way a Richter Scale is efficient. Second, compressive scales represent quantities according to relevance. When something is scarce, such as bananas in winter time, being able to discriminate between the quantities one and two matters. On the other hand, there is no fitness relevance to being able to distinguish between high numbers such as 280 and 281 bananas. Third, ecologic features such as distance to a predator or prey present themselves to our sensory systems in compressive scales. Imagine a line of trees in a forest; trees closer to us appear farther apart from each other than trees that are far from us. Those in closer proximity will impact our fitness more than those farther away. Finally, everything in nature occurs through recursion of underlying "rules of nature." As such, everything natural is compounding, a phenomenon better expressed on compressive scales than on linear scales.

However, linear scales (equidistance between every consecutive numbers) serve a transactional world better than compressive scales. From a counterparty transaction perspective, high resolution at high numbers matters even more than at lower numbers. For example, spending $25,000 for a car versus $24,000 is a huge discrepancy for a customer with a net worth of $30,000. It is vital that the consumer "senses" the $1,000 difference. A linear scale enables this sensing far better than a compressive scale.

It is intuitively appealing to speculate that the emergence of linear notational systems for numbers in the modern world in multiple cultures, including India, Assyria, Sumer, Rome, and China, was a function of the rising counterparty risk in transactions associated with the transition from a high-alignment world to a

---

114.   See https://www.amazon.com/Compound-Thinking-Joon-Yun-ebook/dp/B015GCMHFC/ref=s-r_1_1?ie=UTF8&qid=1547931605&sr=8-1&keywords=compound+thinking+joon+yun.

low-alignment world. Specifically, the development of linear scales catalyzed trade among counterparties (reciprocal altruism).

Indeed, the oldest known human systems for counting—the invention of the small clay tokens in the Zagros region of Iran around 4000 BCE,[115] the pictographs on tablets representing numerals in 3500 BCE,[116] and the abstract numerals dissociated from the thing being counted in 3100 BCE[117]—are thought to have been developed to facilitate transactions of commodities.[118] Soon thereafter, Sumerians invented arithmetic, including addition, subtraction, multiplication, and division, to manage their grain trade.[119] Thereafter, more and more advanced mathematics began to emerge.[120]

There is no doubt that linear mathematics has proven its worth. High resolution at high numbers is the only way to create the kind of precision at high numbers that would allow us to land a rocket on a faraway moon. On the other hand, the near complete hegemony of linear-scale mathematics over compressive-scale mathematics also comes with a significant social cost. All natural phenomena occur through the recursion of underlying fundamentals, resulting in compounding outcomes. Linear-scale mathematics is poor at capturing and studying compounding phenomena, which happens everywhere in the natural world.

Notice that everything in nature curves, and all the straight lines you see are man-made.

Humans relying on linear-scale mathematics tend to significantly underestimate the compounding effects of growth as well as decline, which would be

---

115. See http://en.finaly.org/index.php/Two_precursors_of_writing:_plain_and_complex_tokens.
116. Schmandt-Besserat, D. (1996). *How writing came about.* Austin: University of Texas Press.
117. Schmandt-Besserat, *How writing came about.*
118. See https://en.wikipedia.org/wiki/History_of_ancient_numeral_systems.
119. Nissen, H. J., Damerow, P., & Englund, R. (1993). *Archaic bookkeeping.* Chicago: University of Chicago Press.
120. See, for example, https://en.wikipedia.org/wiki/Topology.

far better gauged on compressive scales. Black swans tend to get underpriced as a result.

On a final note, philosophers have long debated the role of language in our ability to experience the world. Gorgias of Leontini posited that the physical world cannot be experienced except through language. Plato and St. Augustine believed that words were merely labels applied to already existing concepts. Immanuel Kant believed language was one of many tools used by humans to experience the world.

In recent times, the theory of linguistic relativity (also known as the Sapir-Whorf hypothesis) has emerged to posit that individuals experience the world based on the language they habitually use. For example, because there was a paucity of color terminology in Homeric Greek literature, Greeks at the time are presumed not to have experienced colors as we can today.[121]

Thus, if the shift from high-alignment kin-based social systems to low-alignment systems was a catalyst for the development of elaborate languages, then the same fundamental shift of our social evolution may also have had a hand in helping us experience the world in a far richer fashion and develop advanced thoughts.

In short, the fall from the Eden of our tribal past may have precipitated the development of human awareness, instead of the other way around. (In the standard version of the story, humans were expelled from Eden for eating an apple that led to awareness.)

A broader interpretation of the theory of linguistic relativity suggests that naming words promotes consciousness through awareness. By transitivity, those who espouse such a view could make the case that the transition of human social systems from inclusive fitness to reciprocal altruism may have been a forcing function for the emergence of human consciousness.

---

121. See https://en.wikipedia.org/wiki/Linguistic_relativity_and_the_color_naming_debate.

From an individual life's perspective, children have no subjective memory of the time before they could name things. Fractally, from the perspective of the species, humans have no recorded memory of the time before the emergence of symbolic systems.

Memetic Parallax and Mob Mentality

Right about now, we should start talking about how humanity's path forward is to overcome divisions, replace discord with harmony, and find the spirit of oneness that unites us as a species.

That's not going to happen—either for this book or for humanity.

Why? Do we as authors have a dark view of humanity's future? Do we believe that humanity is doomed to endless conflict?

No.

The reason is far simpler: binary divisions, either/or choices, and various types of polarization aren't a bug of human social software. They're a feature.

Think about it.

What comes immediately after "world peace"? Civil war.

Again, why? Humans tend to form groups that disagree with each other, just as a single cell must divide through the process of mitosis to enable the growth of an organism.

From a multilevel selection perspective,[122] evolution selects for systems with features that increase evolutionary capacity: imperfect replication, sexual reproduction, predation, programmed death, memetics, etc. Add to this list "memetic

---

122. Wilson, D. S. (2015). *Does altruism exist? Culture, genes, and the welfare of others*. New Haven, CT: Yale University Press.

parallax," which is the tendency of meme groups to diverge into competing views.[123]

The tendency toward groupthink driven by memetic algorithms can trap systems in local minima in the adaptive landscape that impede evolutionary novelty and constrain fitness. From a multilevel selection perspective, a certain degree of trait (meme or physical) diversity and conflict within a system promotes system robustness and evolutionary capacity. The propensity to disagree with others—many incentives and disincentives influence the process—can promote overall system fitness. Indeed, at a macro level, the theory of evolutionary capacity predicts that selection favors systems that generate feature parallax (diversity over consensus), especially when it promotes conflict to a degree that optimizes competition and accelerates evolution. For example:

Predator-prey competition can be viewed as a feature parallax that promotes conflict of interests, competition with high reward (energy) and punishment (necrosis), and increased evolutionary capacity. Cambrian radiation (diversity, speciation) resulted from a period of particularly robust runaway predator-prey coevolution, which involved a Darwinian arms race for features related to mobility, evasion, defense, perception, weapons, communication, social behaviors, and further evolutionary novelty. Predator-prey coevolution is an example of active, adverse selection of traits for the prey and positive selection for predators.

When there is trust, respect, and alignment (genetic and otherwise) between individuals or groups, the parallax can be highly beneficial to the individuals and to the overall combined superorganism. A second opinion from a trusted partner is a significant value-add in partnerships, teams, and marriages.

Sexual reproduction is a system feature that promotes genotype and phenotype parallax (male vs. female). The parallax is associated with collaboration as well as conflict of interest between the sexes (intersexual competition, asymmetric parental investment, etc.) and intrasexual competition. The competing agendas promote vast increases in novel features, including cognition and social behaviors.

---

123. Socratic dialogues and Hegelian dialectic both reflect the fundamental role of memetic parallax in human inquiry. See Hegel, G. W. F. (2018). *The phenomenology of spirit*. Oxford, UK: Oxford University Press.

Sexual reproduction is an example of active, positive selection for traits among gender counterparties with highly aligned interest in the joint venture (i.e., offspring) in which each have 50 percent insider interest (or less for males, given paternal uncertainty).[124]

The "free market" is an economic system that instantiates parallax maximization: conflict of interests, competition, and asymmetric rewards (economic benefit). Observed through a wider lens, the fragmentation of socio-political-economic philosophies—including socialism and capitalism—recapitulates, at the higher fractal level, the tendency toward memetic parallax. These parallaxed philosophies compete for members.

When Balkanization occurs, individuals and groups also tend to unify internally, merge, form meme alliances, and cooperate—again, many incentives and disincentives influence the process—to compete against outside groups. When facing a common external enemy, we tend to settle our internal disputes and unite against the enemy until a larger consensus (peace) results.[125]

Once the enemy is dissipated, memetic parallax reemerges. The victors of WWII entered peace discussions with a spirit of international cooperation and exited with divergent agendas. There's wisdom to the notion that a war defending humanity against a common enemy such as an alien invasion would diffuse existing ideological stalemates, at least until the victory parade.

When a group Balkanizes into many groups, an important second trait of social systems deters further fragmentation—the hive mentality. From a total-system evolutionary-capacity perspective, there is a tradeoff: parallax is preferred over consensus, but continued parallax and over-fragmentation are also costly. "Us versus them" campaigns require retaining and growing the "us." Social systems are wired to consolidate and grow their membership and power as superorganisms.

---

124. The standard explanation for why sexual reproduction evolved was increased diversity. We propose a more salient reason: that vested interest in our offspring is a powerful driver of the careful and motivated selection of our reproductive partner's traits.

125. The rise of nationalism following the unification of warring factions in Japan instigated imperialism—a pattern repeated often around the world when clans settle their differences in favor of common aims. Imperialism and colonialism are outlets that feed the beast and keep internal harmony between warring tribes.

The competing effects of groupthink and memetic divergence mitigates the over- and under-Balkanization of groups, respectively, and reflect a fitness tradeoff. Selection favors dynamic systems capable of both consensus memetics and memetic parallax in a context-dependent fashion. A fractal is apparent. Evolution favors systems with capacity for two features that are themselves in competitive parallax: the tendency for groupthink and the tendency for parallax.

Thus, the arcs of human and evolutionary histories are poised to teeter between competition and cooperation in a never-ending vacillation across the different scales of biology and time. Peace will follow war, and war will follow peace. And so on.[126]

So far we have spoken favorably of the hive mentality. Under certain conditions, however, hive mentality can be transformed into its dangerous alter-ego: mob mentality.

In her treatise on the psychology of moral panics, Dr. Maia Newley explores the innate vulnerability of human communities to mass hysteria: even well-educated and apparently rational intellectuals (Hobbes, Bacon, Milton, Locke) were not immune to joining the broad public in becoming convinced that evil witches with great powers were imperiling England.[127]

126. Parallax can occur along the temporal axis, rather than only at any one moment in time. Hegelian dialectic—and to some extent the entire intellectual history of Marxism—is built on this. Dualities that evolve over time—the cyclical procession of thesis, antithesis, and synthesis—delineate the progress of human society. Now, of course, the absurdity of Hegel was his announcement that the early 19th century was the termination of this historical procession of thesis, antithesis, and synthesis. Others, too, have tried to make similar claims. Francis Fukuyama wrote in *The End of History and the Last Man* (1992) that the neoclassical liberal state was the end of history. All of that is juxtaposed against the capitalist model, where progress is the persistent story of heroic individuals overcoming adversaries. But neither Marxism nor capitalism can lay total claim to the progress of humanity. It's not just either agency or context. It's both. But it doesn't really matter if this is the end of history, if this is the final synthesis, or if this is just the next stage. The point is that it is the imminent next thing; it's the thing that's already happening. We're not creating it. We're describing it, and in describing it we're part of it. We usher in this new era that may be imminent. But we do it in a conscious way, and that consciousness really makes all the difference. That's what this book is about: not just finding our way home but doing so with consciousness.
127. See https://www.academia.edu/10664162/_Abstract_The_Jacobean_Witch_Craze_-_The_Case_ for_Folie_A_Plusieurs_Psychopathology_of_early_modern_folk_devils_and_moral_panics_.

Such mass hysteria can occur at any scale of social aggregation. For example, Ekbom's syndrome is a delusional disorder in which individuals incorrectly believe they are infested with parasites, often compulsively gathering "evidence" to present to others. Pairs of people also can famously exhibit mob mentality.[128] For example, folie à deux is when two people, typically a patient and a spouse, share such a delusion, cultivating an "us-versus-them" attitude that can lead to magnificent triumphs or to Bonnie-and-Clyde-like calamities. In folie à plusieurs, large groups share a delusion and selectively aggregate the "evidence" that supports their collective belief. Witch hunts fall into this category.[129]

So, are witch hunts a thing of the past? Hardly. Groupthink—including its most extreme form, mob mentality—is another evolutionarily selected feature (not a bug) of living systems that is not going away anytime soon. Moreover, as a consequence of the increasing interconnectedness to which we have referred repeatedly in this book, we are more vulnerable to mob behavior than ever in the post-technology age.

Whether looked at in terms of folie à plusieurs, folie à deux, or the tendency of large groups to undertake witch hunts, groupthink seems pathological at best and deeply destructive at worst. So what is the upside? Can groupthink offer greater promise for humanity than the (false) hope of "world peace?"

We started this book discussing the powerful coordinating force of genetic proximity and Hamilton's rule. The existence of Hamilton's rule allowed family tribes to evolve, eventually becoming kin-based clans and villages. In this way, biological (genetic) algorithms shared across individuals have enabled us as humans to coordinate our collective behaviors as a "superorganism" that transcends individual boundaries.

What is true of genetic affinity also turns out to be true of memetic affinity. Genetic affinity creates the motivation for individuals to coordinate behaviors

128. Being madly in love can be seen as an example of a shared delusion.
129. See http://www.academia.edu/10664162/_Abstract_The_Jacobean_Witch_Craze_-_The_Case_for_Folie_A_Plusieurs_Psychopathology_of_early_modern_folk_devils_and_moral_panics_.

as a group "superorganism"; memetic affiliation creates the common language that allows groups to function as groups, rather than as collections of individuals. In this way, "groupthink" is an evolutionary win for both the individual and the superorganism. Rearing offspring, shared defense, resource acquisition, migration, and communication all work better in a kin-based group. We would call memetic affiliation in prehistoric times "tribal beliefs"; we might call memetic affiliation today "corporate culture" or "patriotism." The root is the same: our power to communicate, coordinate, and learn—the essence of our evolutionary advantage as a social species. Without groupthink, we—all of us—quite simply would not exist.

For the foregoing reasons, groupthink is clearly a feature of human evolution. The problem comes—as we have seen repeatedly in this book—when this and other evolutionary advantages become liabilities in our dizzyingly global and interconnected world away from kin tribes. Evolutionary dislocations can render our propensity for groupthink into a bug, especially when memetic algorithms reflect the interests of others besides those of the people in the group.

Humans belong to many groups with lower degrees of genetic alignment. Criteria for inclusion in such groups are highly varied and include factors such as choice (marriage or friendship), admission (college), coercion (military draft), serendipity (public bus riders), among many others. Some groups are transient (a dinner party), while others are enduring (alumni). Some groups are offline (a book club), while others live online (a hashtag community). Some groups are based on physical characteristics (left-handed or blue eyes), while others are based on beliefs, preferences, or common experience (church, fandom, neighborhood, nation, political affiliation, language, clubs, brands, Twitter followers, etc.). Other examples of groups include sports teams, schools, cults, unions, companies, gangs, countries, ethnic groups, mafias, neighborhoods, speakers of a particular language, or Facebook friends of a particular person. All groups are inclusive of ingroups by exclusion of others (outgroup).[130]

As technology increases information liquidity, the role of memetic algorithms in coordinating human group behaviors through all of these categories is rising relative to that of genetic alignment. On the one hand, new types of useful communities can form by virtue of all the technology-enabled connectivity.

But on the other hand, there is a dark side. In the context of low alignment, rising counterparty risk, and high connectivity, it has never been easier for the human tendency to form groups to be hijacked by memetic algorithms to serve interests other than the interests of the people. The increasing connectivity enables memetic algorithms to capture human minds far and wide via telecommunication technologies and turn these collections of individual minds into self-dealing, nefarious memetic superorganisms (self-expanding beasts). Most significantly, the agency of memetic superorganisms can overtake the agency of the individuals that comprise the superorganism.

In some cases, individuals' surrender of agency to the interest of superorganisms is benign (such as being a Chicago Cubs fan). Other times, this surrender can be nefarious (cults). Of the latter cases, individuals' inability to withdraw from the stranglehold of the superorganism-beast becomes a serious issue. At that point, mob mentality of the superorganism can own the minds of the individuals, who lose their capacity for intellectual honesty (the hallmark of someone under the spell of a dangerous mob).

Systemic fear is the most common trigger for individuals to surrender their personal agency in service of groupthink. In the Darwinian calculus, fearful individuals join groups (superorganisms) in order to increase individual fitness. "Mobs" are extreme versions of these fear-driven groups.[131] Malevolent actors have

130. Imagine managing the invitations for a kids' party in a class of 60 kids. Every kid that is added to the invitation list paradoxically increases the degree of exclusion felt by remaining outgroup members. Inclusion can have unexpected exclusionary effects, and exclusion can have an unexpected inclusionary impact on the ingroup (such as the vow of marriage).
131. Here are some strategies for dealing with potentially nefarious mobs. Start by cataloging all the potentially mob-like groups we belong to: family, friends, workers, belief systems, organizations, clubs, affiliations, preferences, characteristics, hobbies, etc. For each mob-like group we belong to, assess whether our agency

increasing opportunities to hijack our natural inclination to act (positively and productively) in the service of larger groups, stoking mob anxieties and thereby increasingly our vulnerability to Bonnie-and-Clyde-like implosions of various types.[132]

Examples abound. A relatively benign one is the tendency of parents of children's sports teams to believe that the referee's calls are unfairly going against their own team. A less benign example is the rising degree of confirmation bias and polarization between political groups in the United States from 2016 to the present. Both examples demonstrate how the innate tendency to seek confirmation bias serves the interests of the group: the superorganism strengthens itself at the expense of individual intellectual autonomy and accentuates the degree of polarization among outgroups. Heightened polarization can increase the degree of fear, thereby increasing the susceptibility to confirmation bias and ingroup groupthink, which exacerbates polarization in a self-reinforcing fashion.

Groupthink and mob behavior are everywhere. They are a defining feature of life and subconsciously influence our everyday behavior far more than we realize.

---

has been co-opted by a mob mentality. Specifically try to assess (may need third-party help) whether overt or subtle peer pressure to conform, or a desire to enter or maintain membership in a group, is influencing our beliefs, assumptions, behaviors and our ability to gather evidence without bias. Be aware if our fear of losing membership in various mobs or our greed for gaining status in various mobs (ex: getting into an elite college) is influencing our behaviors and thought patterns. We can try removing ourselves from mobs or seeking help. We can make an effort to become more aware of the mob mentality in people around us. In particular, we can assess whether a person is cherry-picking information to support their existing beliefs. If so, the person may be under the influence of a mob mentality on that issue. We can each try to attenuate the mob effect in the people around us by bypassing their mental blocks using tools such as humor or music.

132.   Mobbing, then, is a form of group behavior in which ingroup members exhibit aggression toward outgroup members or non-conforming ingroup members. The adaptive value of mobbing could be examined at the level of the individual and the superorganism. Interstrata competition is the conflict of interests between the adaptive agendas of a superorganism and its individual components. Biologists have debated whether evolutionary selection of group behaviors occurs at the level of the group (Konrad Lorenz), the individual (John Maynard), or at multiple levels (David Wilson and Edward Wilson). Ironically, the aggressive censure of "group selection" advocates by mainstream biologists exemplifies mob mentality. Trying to understand the behavior of mobs through the behavior of individuals alone is akin to trying to understand human behavior through the behavior of cells alone. When it comes to mobbing, it may be more illuminating to simultaneously contemplate the behavior from the perspective of the individuals and the mob as a superorganism.

Although we originated in tightly aligned collaborative kin tribes, the combined effects of memetic parallax and mob mentality enable the superorganism to self-replicate into a collection of units that are collaborative within ingroups (a nuclear family or a kin tribe) and competitive among an array of outgroups. Superorganisms are characterized by diversity among competing outgroups that are internally collaborative. Said more briefly, a separate peace, not peace, is the resulting dynamic reality.[133]

It seems some balance of competing interests and alignment of interests within social groups maximizes evolutionary fitness.

———————

Here is a recap. First, the evolutionary emergence of these traits did not anticipate an era in which competing groups could arm themselves with advanced weaponry—including weapons of mass destruction (nuclear weapons) and weapons of mass distortion (extractive media). Diversity without common ground creates separatism. Separatism with mob mentality promotes polarization. Polarization plus advanced weaponry leads to upheaval. Now, the tendencies of human social groups to exhibit memetic parallax and mobbing may have been rendered maladaptive in the modern context due to evolutionary dislocations.

Second, evolution did not anticipate an era in which memetic superorganisms could form around memes that serve the interests of a superorganism itself but not serve the interests of the individuals that comprise the superorganism. This distinction is important. A beehive is a memetic mob. The Waggle Dance to share the story of where to find food serves the interest of the hive and the individuals in the hive.

Now, external counterparties, such as a self-dealing company trying to maximize short-term profits at the expense of customers, can lure the public into

---

133. In John Knowles' novel *A Separate Peace*, the protagonist Gene "discovered that his private evil, which caused him to hurt Phineas, is the same evil—only magnified—that results in war."

forming mobs that benefit the company, even if the benefit to the people in the group is unclear. This is effectively the branding function of many companies.

The phenomenon of memetic mobs under the control of external counter-parties is not limited to companies. Think of political or social propaganda. Think of the political correctness movement. Sometimes there is not even a human obviously involved in hijacking the mindshare of human groups. Some fads just come and go for reasons that seem inexplicable.

Here are the overarching questions resulting from this chapter. How do we as individuals (and as groups) act to turn groupthink back into a positive factor in human evolution? How can we turn our competing propensities to fracture and form hives into forces for good?

In our view, the revolution begins with aligning our interest with others.

Reimagining Fairy Tales

Humanity is trapped in a cycle. The institutions we built to attack the self-expanding beasts in one era became the self-expanding beasts of the next. Along the way, we have made great strides in the collective quality of life on the planet. Yet, despite all of those advances and the combined cognitive capacities of over seven billion human minds at work every day to create the future in one way or another, there is a growing dread about where the world is headed.

In this book, we argued for what we believe is the change that will matter most: restoring the alignment of interest in our communities. We proposed the development of interdependent stakeholding through innovations such as Blockchain and cultural reprogramming to promote self-driving revolutions that will steward the world to a better place.

But we saved one more strategy for discussion here—a secret weapon in our battle to overcome our default programming: the fairy tale.

Fairy tales are our way back to our source code. Fairy tales are the shadows of our instincts.

We hereby present a perspective on the evolution of fairy tales through the same primary lens we have used throughout this book—the evolution of human social systems from high alignment to low alignment.

First, we note that fairy tales—and folk stories in general—were memetically selected to promote the evolutionary fitness of human kin hives.

Second, we claim that the marketplace—the evolutionary selection regime—for fairy tales became distorted by the same factor that distorted all of human social behaviors: the loss of vested interest among storytellers and story-listeners that previously had been protected within kin hives.

Third, we claim that the most popular fairy tales today represent survivor bias toward the most commodified and sellable stories of the human experience. These commodified stories may benefit the kin tribe in some ways but may harm it in other ways.

Fourth, we will attempt to reconstruct what a fairy tale might have looked like in the Pleistocene Age, when the kin hive was the prevailing social system for humans.[134] This was an era before the existence of written language; there's no such thing as a fossil record of oral stories. We will attempt to reverse-engineer the fairy tale of that era using the single assumption that, before the shift from solidarity to solitary, the rise of separatism, the "Tinderification" of relationships, and the commodification of human effort, we lived in tightly aligned kin hives.

Why do stories exist?

Stories are valuable in promoting evolutionary fitness from a multilevel selection perspective. As memes, they differ from genes in their capacity to transfer behavioral traits. For example, memetic transfer of poisonous food avoidance has advantages over the selection and transfer of that trait via gene-based, hardwired food preferences. Story memes are more efficient than genes in transferring traits horizontally within a generation and vertically across generations, even across great gaps of space and time. It is little surprise, then, that selection favored the coevolution of storytelling and story-listening as companion biological programs to enable the memetic transmission of stories in human social systems.

It is easy to see how a folk tale can help convey useful principles in a way that promotes fitness within a tribe. For example, the death of a parent is one of the most transformative moments in the evolutionary fitness of their offspring. In the prehistoric age, the probability of losing one or both parents during one's childhood was not insubstantial. One would predict that the folk tales in the tribal age

---

134. A geological epoch that lasted from about 2,588,000 to 11,700 years ago.

might have addressed the topic of losing a parent. One might even predict that folktales back then would portray another woman—perhaps an aunt—stepping in for a deceased mom.

Let's now discuss how stories might evolve as tribal needs evolve.

Think about a story as an organism (or a virus). Stories, like organisms, evolve. Imagine a tree that represented the arborization of a story over the generations—a history of his (or her) story before the time of written words, when only oral traditions existed.

As stories arborize through retelling, they mutate. The diverse versions of a particular story compete among themselves for audience attention. The later generations of a story may share a common origin, but they are not codependent on each other for survival the way the branches of a tree are. Thus, the evolutionary selection of mutating stories operates on survival through competition. The loudest chick in the nest gets the attention.

In the kin tribe era, the genetic alignment between storytellers and story-listeners incentivized the selection of stories that best served the interests of the tribe. Over the course of human evolution, however, the same phenomenon that affected the evolution of human social systems affected the evolution of stories. As we became more mobile and our vested interest in each other declined, the way stories were used also changed.

That is, instead of telling a story in the best interests of the listener, people started to tell stories to promote their own interests. The shift to a low-alignment world incentivized the commodification of stories—where the purpose of stories shifts from inherent value to external (promotional) value. Think of every Facebook post ever.

In the context of commodification, the natural dynamic of the marketplace for stories is a race to the bottom: whatever sells best at the time. As such, stories tend to hijack the human storytelling/story-listening neural pathways to serve themselves. In a way, stories themselves become self-expanding superorganisms—or memetic beasts.

In today's low-alignment society, the line of defense against these beasts has been breached. Once kin genetic alignment is gone and the defenses are down, the co-evolution of stories, storytellers, and story-listeners selects for the high fructose corn syrup of stories and storytellers. Commodified stories are pouring in, sweeping up children and adults—tranquilized by "feel good" hooks and other appealing devices—into the belly of the beast.

Remember, once corrupted, the system selects for the most exploitative version of itself. The story industry has optimized the hooks to maximize attention, which in and of itself is not evil. But the intention to use these hooks to serve their own interests at the expense of the people is the nefarious force. Be wary of such self-dealing storytellers, their accomplices, and their industries: entertainment, publishing, podcasts, media, speaker series, etc.

But most of all, we should be wary of the stories themselves. Once the memetic superorganisms are in charge, the system self-selects for the most egregious violations of the story market. That is, the race-to-the-bottom nature of the misaligned systems induces ongoing mutations of stories toward commercial success rather than service to the community.

With this sobering perspective in mind, let's examine the love story template with a keen sense of suspicion that they are commodified versions of earlier stories which were bastardized to serve and perpetuate the beast. The most famous love story in the modern age is about self-involved lovers whose fates are misaligned with that of their communities. William Shakespeare took that woe-is-us, us-against-the-world narrative and made Romeo and Juliet the most commercially successful love story ever.

Now, imagine instead a primordial love story about lovers whose fates are aligned with that of their communities. Did such a love story ever exist?

Once upon a time, approximately a thousand years ago, a ritual of courtly love emerged in Europe after eons of cultural and monastic oppression against romance.[135] A few centuries later, the ritual disappeared just as quickly as it had appeared, leaving in its wake countless ballads and legends.

The ritual of courtly love was spread by the lyrics of troubadours and encoded in the archetypal hero narrative. While the variants are vast in number, they have in common a basic structure. A suitor becomes attracted to a lady. He worships her from afar and declares his passionate devotion. The lady virtuously and steadfastly rejects the suitor. The suitor responds with renewed wooing with oaths of virtue, eternal fealty, and moans of approaching death from lovesickness. He pursues heroic deeds of honor and valor. He slays the beast. He returns, ennobled by combat. The lady swoons. Consummation ensues. The fairy tale ends, and happily ever after begins.

The standards for consent today are considerably lower.

The key features of courtly love are honor, sacrifice, chivalry, service, and valor—ideals that are viewed with skepticism, if not laugh-out-loud derision, in today's culture. In the ideal of courtly love, however, these sacrificial features are expressed unsarcastically and unconditionally. The lady virtuously rejects her suitor without any guarantee that he will return, dead or alive. At no point does she insist that her suitor embark on a Hero's Journey or attempt to improve her own lot at the expense of his sacrifice. At no point does she ask him to slay the beast.

For his part, the suitor embarks on the Hero's Journey on his own volition with no guarantee of surviving the contest with the beast or winning the lady's heart. His heroic and honorable deeds are done in the name of the people, and not in the name of the lady or his self-interest. Like the lady's, his sacrifice is in service of the greater good.[136]

While these archetypal stories of courtly love told by the troubadours may seem like quaint relics of a long-ago forgotten time, they actually express enduring biological fundamentals. Whatever the everyday behavior of men might suggest to the contrary, a hero instinct is deeply embedded in the male psyche and encoded

---

135. See https://en.wikipedia.org/wiki/Courtly_love.
136. Virtue for its own sake and not it's signaling value.

in male genes. If an act that might cost his life is offset by the fitness gain of other individuals multiplied by their respective degrees of genetic relatedness, the sacrificial act enhances his inclusive fitness. The same math applies to the female instinct to nurture and defend. However, female fecundity is a rate-limiting step of evolution and, mathematically speaking, the sacrifice of a male is on average less costly than a fecund female's. The "heroism" of men in striking out to slay beasts and otherwise prove their valor is a function of their (our) evolutionary expendability.

The fundamental point is that, in the ongoing drama of biological evolution, females do more than procreate: they choose. A key female contribution to evolutionary progress is trait selection through mate choice. From a Darwinian perspective, the benefit of sexual selection is not merely an increase in progeny diversity—the accepted wisdom in evolutionary theory. Sexual selection also increases evolutionary capacity by enabling the active, positive selection of beneficial traits in a joint venture (a child) in which each party has up to 50 percent vested genetic interest (males, statistically, have less than 50 percent vested interest in the joint venture due to paternal uncertainty).

When layering the mythology of courtly love over the evolutionary biology of female mate choice, it becomes apparent that females hold enormous power: they not only can help surface genetically wired instincts of valor and service in males, they can also actively help select those genetically encoded traits for the propagation of her lineage.

So, was the era of courtly love merely a period of aberration? Or was it a glimpse of a deeper collective subconsciousness? The cult following that surrounds the 1987 Rob Reiner film The Princess Bride is just one indicator that our medieval past remains, subconsciously, part of our present.[137]

---

137. Current concerns about everyone spending too much time staring at small screens has induced a nostalgia for the quaint era when everyone stared at screens larger than the largest creature to walk the earth. Lights were down, and speaker volumes were up to make sure no one other than the storyteller could be seen or heard, such as the couple in heat in row 27. Everyone else sat looking tranquilized—eyes glued to the eye candy on the wall and shoes glued to the shoe candy on the floor. Regrettably, much of the would-be shoe candy would be intercepted by mouths, lured by high-fructose corn syrup and other industrial ingredients, designed by formerly underpaid PhDs, to separate you from your after-tax dollars. These ingredient "hooks"

Is it possible that the ritual of courtly love was also a fairy tale of the prehistoric kin tribe era? If so, can our genetically encoded instincts for honor and valor be surfaced to the behavioral level in the context of proper cultural norms? Can today's new generation of troubadours and storytellers socially engineer modern day heroes through song and stories to take on the stampede of self-expanding beasts?

In our view, these are the central questions of the day for the storytelling industries.

Now we are going to unpack the other folk tale template that dominates the modern story economy: the Hero's Journey.

First, a brief background on the template. The common patterns of the hero myth have been explored by many scholars, including Edward Burnett Tylor, Otto Rank, Lord Raglan, and Carl Jung. The Hero's Journey is a particular framing of the hero myth popularized in modern scholarship by Joseph Campbell. In The Hero with a Thousand Faces, Campbell described the basic narrative pattern as follows:

A hero ventures forth from the world of common day into a region of supernatural wonder: fabulous forces are there encountered and a decisive victory is won: the hero comes back from this mysterious adventure with the power to bestow boons on his fellow man.[138]

In his Masks of God series, for example, Campbell deconstructs the myth of Beowulf, a hero who takes on beasts in the form of Grendel, Grendel's mother, and

---

were given incrementally more acceptable titles, such as Goobers, and sold at monopolistic prices at cultural economic institutions affectionately, and "confectionately," known as the *concession stand*.

They were never clear on exactly who was conceding to whom. As they say, if you don't know who the mark is, it's probably you. It turns out that, as with every element of this carnival-looking-for-marks, the word *concession* is an extraction masquerading as a service to you. All that said, boy do we love going to the movies! They really are a nice escape. Especially those Hero's Journeys. They are a nice escape from the rest of the zombie-dystopia reality. It's just like the vicious cycle of Ritalin and ADHD causing the existence of the other. When you are fully immersed in the beast, that's the last thing you are aware of.

138. Campbell, J. (1949). *The hero with a thousand faces*. Princeton, NJ: Princeton University Press, p. 23.

a dragon to bring the boon of security to his village.[139] Joseph Campbell believed in the use of myths by later civilizations, including ours, to express humanity's desire to make the world "transparent to transcendence." Myths have the power to express the inexpressible—things that existed before and beyond words. He regarded transcendence as something that ensues after recognizing that the world of phenomena is a merely an expression of an underlying eternal source.

So right about now, this book should start talking how we need to find the hero that lies deep within. "We must reconnect with our genes for honor and valor," we might be saying now.

That's not going to happen here. That's not the point we're trying to make. If anything, we have no shortage of Hero's Journey stories. We also have no shortage of people who are obsessed with slaying beasts—particularly those self-expanding institutional beasts that have managed to swallow us alive.

We are now going to discuss how the Hero's Journey itself is a self-expanding beast that undermines our very efforts to take on the stampede of self-expanding beast.

———————————

Is it possible that the Hero's Journey is not only not the solution to the unfolding current dystopia but is a contributor to it? Is the obsession with one's own journey, and our self-identification with the hero-protagonist, just another manifestation of narcissism? After all, Joseph Campbell described the Hero's Journey as a point of inspiration for the self-help movement.[140] What if the cumulative effect of the millions of self-satisfying Hero's Journeys is exactly what got us to this point of collective dysfunction?

Do we need a completely different kind of hero's story?

Earlier in the book, we also asked why human social institutions have consistently evolved from high-minded, high-alignment origins to self-dealing,

139. See https://twitter.com/ImBrittanyEvans/status/1065740137710190594.
140. See https://en.wikipedia.org/wiki/Hero%27s_journey#Self-help_movement_and_therapy.

low-alignment maturity.[141] Certainly it was not due to a lack of trying by the (heroic) pioneers who created the institutions and, later, by the (comparably) heroic reformers who attempted to change them. At that point we argued that such attempts to slay beasts (self-dealing institutions) were no match for the race-to-the-bottom evolutionary pressures feeding those beasts.

But now we ask a different question: could it be that centuries of Hero's Journeys—Beowulf versus Grendel, St. George versus the dragon, Mr. Smith versus Washington—have actually been part of the problem all along?

Worse yet, what if it turns out that, in this ages-old story, we are not Beowulf but Grendel? What if we are the anti-hero? Rather than awakening in the belly of the beast, what if it turns out that we collectively comprise the beast? That would be a rude awakening.

If we are meant to be the foil of someone else's Hero's Journey, what would the Beast's

Journey look like? As Grendel, we are hungry and people are delicious. People don't go down easy, so we have to pick our spots. Now people have this device called the Hero's Journey that encourages boys and girls to act like heroes and slay us.

At some point, the system self-selects for a character named Beowulf. He is apparently some hero and wants to take it out on us as part of his transformation. He also wants to save the world.

In this reversed version of the standard Hero's Journey, the Beast's Journey is to support the Hero's Journey of someone else. The only problem is, the way the story is scripted, Beowulf's Hero's Journey is to kill us, the beast. In the end we die so that Beowulf can go home as the hero. That's not such a great outcome. John Gardner wrote a version of this story called Grendel. And there is a mutated version of Gardner's story in which the beast not only lives but gets the

141. See https://books.google.com/books?hl=en&lr=&id=HFHpCAAAQBAJ&oi.

girl. La Belle et la Bête (Beauty and the Beast) is a fairy tale written by French novelist Gabrielle-Suzanne Barbot de Villeneuve and published in 1740.[142]

––––––––––––––

There are two key features of the Hero's Journey folk tale templates that give us pause.

First, in the Hero's Journey template, the good and bad qualities are typically segregated in the characters. In the real world, everybody is a mix of good and bad. In folk tales, people are either good or bad.

Second is the selection of characters that are extreme in their embodiment of good and bad qualities. That is, the characters are painted as black or white instead of grey. The contrived segregation of character archetypes into heroes and beasts is an example.

There is an insidious reason why these features were selected: they maximize audience attention. Who doesn't want the moral convenience of seeing the world through a separatist lens as black and white? Thinking in shades of grey is not easy. The more extreme the archetypes, the easier it is to snack on these stories. The Hero's Journey stories have proven commercially appealing and ubiquitous, rendered with ever cleverer hooks and more fantastic computer-generated effects.

These stories have travelled to all corners of the earth and also across time. Along the way, they have arborized, mutated, and adapted through retranslations that fit the local memetic niche—Odyssey, Beowulf, Star Wars, etc. The Beowulf story alone ramified countless times as the people harboring the story migrated through time and space in Europe. There are the Anglo-Saxon versions, the Germanic versions, and the Scandinavian versions—each with their own set of variants.

What connects all these different stories over space and time is a combination of tropes that comprise the Hero's Journey: the call to adventure, refusal of the call, supernatural aid, crossing the threshold, belly of the whale, road of trials, meeting

142. See https://en.wikipedia.org/wiki/Beauty_and_the_Beast.

with the goddess, woman as temptress, atonement with the father, apotheosis, ultimate boon, refusal of the return, magic flight, rescue from without, return, resurrection, master of two worlds, and return with elixir.

The most important trope, however, is the assignment of roles. The characters are rendered in black and white. Beowulf is the hero-protagonist, and Grendel is assigned the more deviant half of the duality.[143] That's the setup for a widely appealing story. That's the goal of commodification.

In the Hero's Journey, there is a hero and everyone else is a foil to the hero. The Hero's Journey is a self-help narrative that fits the memetic priming induced by rising mutual alienation over the millennia.[144] As people buy into that narrative, the narrative gains strength and size, capturing more hearts in its belly. The coevolution of the story, storytellers, and story-listeners assures its self-expansion.

The story of Beowulf—a self-centered Hero's Journey narrative—is itself a self-expanding beast. The larger story is about how this particular beast of a story, and its descendant story-beasts, diaspora'ed through Europe and devoured mindshare along their voracious paths.

One could make a case that the commodification of the Hero's Journey was a good thing. Surely it's a good thing that the world wakes up to the existence of good and evil.

Not so fast.

The fundamental issue is this: the message that is getting popularized is off the mark. The idea that people are either good or bad is not the reality. In the real world, everyone is a mixed bag of good and bad qualities. Our tendency to think about others through the lens of separatism—a thinking trained and reinforced by the black and white nature of fairy tales—is the foundation of "us versus them" thinking.

143. Grendel is described as descended from the lineage of the biblical figure Cain.
144. As a reminder, when others self-deal, we feel alienated. When we feel alienated, we self-deal. When we self-deal, we alienate others. When they feel alienated, they self-deal. That's a self-reinforcing cycle.

This habit is not only not good; it is the most dangerous trend in the modern world. Polarization through memetic parallax is the existential threat of our time. Worse, the race-to-the-bottom nature of the memetic marketplace selects for the most polarizing versions of stories.

We argue that this phenomenon of corrupted storytelling has been happening since we left the era of kin tribes. However, the phenomenon appears to be accelerating in the modern world. Self-dealing media, including those that use extractive algorithms, are driving the world toward sectionalism, gender wars, race wars, political polarization, witch hunts, and every other type of extremism and mob attack. People are finally beginning to see it.

———————————

In the preceding sections, we made the case that Hero's Journeys are products of the low-alignment era. If so, what was the original Hero's Journey story from which the mutated stories are derived? Is there any way we can find out?

We know there were stories in the prehistoric era before the time of words. On the one hand, we have no record of these stories. On the other hand, as described earlier, we can surmise what those stories might have been, given what we know about the nature of kin hives.

The following framing might help. Joseph Campbell borrowed heavily from Adolf Bastian's concept of the psychic unity of mankind, which is not dissimilar to the modern concept of human groups being a superorganism. Every human mind inherits a decentralized distribution of "elementary ideas," and hence the minds of all people, regardless of their race or culture, operate similarly. According to Bastian, the contingencies of geographic location and historical background engender different local elaborations of the "elementary ideas" he considered these downstream elaborations "folk ideas." For Bastian, the historically conditioned "folk ideas" are of secondary importance to the universal "elementary ideas."[145]

———————————

145. See https://en.wikipedia.org/wiki/Adolf_Bastian#The_Psychic_Unity_of_Mankind.

Importantly, what has changed is this: superorganisms (self-expanding beasts) have sprung up everywhere based on elements other than shared interests among kin (e.g., memetic superorganisms around political beliefs). In these cases, the superorganism can subvert the interests of the people in service of its own self-interest.

In other words, the "folk ideas" apparent in today's folk tales do not serve the interests of humanity. As discussed earlier, the notion that people are either good or evil, rather than shades of grey, is not an elementary truth.

Let's briefly recap what we've discussed so far. Stories once served kin tribes. Once we shifted to low-alignment communities, storytellers' interest shifted to seeking secondary gain for themselves. Stories became commodified. The marketplace for stories started to select for commercial appeal rather than service to the kin tribe. It is this marketplace that selected the Hero's Journey with its simple and appealing archetypes: black and white, evil versus good, beast versus hero.

The Hero's Journey stories are far more self-satisfying than stories that portray us as mixed bags. The former story template has crowded out the latter. Meanwhile, the Hero's Journey story has spread everywhere as a self-replicating beast. In other words, the Hero's Journey is the high fructose corn syrup of stories. We are lured to both by the tip of our tongues.[146]

If the dominant stories we are hearing are the mutated ones, what might be the "elementary ideas" that once served the interest of kin hives? Is there any way to reconstruct the fairy tales of that era?

And why reconstruct this original fairy tale at all? In our view, this fairy tale of the kin tribe era will be an important part of the cultural reprogramming needed to help finish human's transition from the era of kin villages to the global village era. With ten millennia of hindsight to guide us, might humanity at last be able

---

146. Sugar receptors are on the tip of the tongue. Stories also arise from the tip of the tongue.

to escape the seemingly endless game of institutional Whack-a-Mole in which we appear to be trapped? And if we're not to do so as modern-day heroes slaying dragons, then how might we proceed?

If such a story exists, why hasn't it written itself? Why hasn't it been induced by demand? We will explain that shortly. But first we will tell you what we think was the original fairy tale.

That story is not elusive. Like many truths, it's actually hiding in plain sight. We don't need to look further.

If we change one thing from modern fairy tales, the fairy tale of the tribal era emerges from hiding.

So here it is. It requires us to change just one thing: accept that duality is the reality. Each of us is simultaneously the hero and the anti-hero. There is no distinction of subjectivity between Beowulf and Grendel. There is no separatism of black and white. We are all grey.

Imagine if the aim of our journey is to steward each other's journeys. We believe this was the fairy tale of the kin tribe era. We believe this was the original love story. We believe this was also the original Hero's Journey. We are never just the hero or just the anti-hero; we are a hybrid of the two. Beowulf and Grendel return home together, and there is no separate assignment of a better or worse ending to either part.

Is ice cream the worst evil perpetrated by Big Food, a recipe for childhood diabetes? Or the best food ever, as children attest? The truth is, ice cream is just ice cream. Whether ice cream is good or bad is a matter of the observer's perspective, which means it's both. A curse is a gift. Just look at the hundred-year loyalty of the Chicago Cubs fans. A gift is a curse. Just look at fate of most lottery winners. Was Mother Teresa's selflessness selfish? As much as we want to disassociate, there are two sides of the same coin.

Anakin Skywalker is Darth Vader. But to sell tickets, they had to be displayed as two separate characters spread out over years of sequels—as the hero or the villain, not the hero and the villain. Is it a feature or a bug that food, travel, or a movie can activate our neural reward reflex? The reality is yes—as in yes, it's both. Holding competing moral thoughts is not easy.

The only reality that doesn't exist is the story that there is a good that is separate from evil. Angel versus the devil. Superman versus Lex Luthor. Yet these are the stories that sell tickets and travel far.[147]

On the other hand, the "original" fairy tale (in our view) of the tribal era—that all of us embody the duality of being both good and evil, and that our Hero's Journeys are to stewards each other's journeys—has no intrinsic appeal as a story. It has no commercial value. Therefore, it's an untellable story. If this was easy to sell, it would have been told already and widely sold.

The human mind has trouble accepting that duality is our reality. Our brain tends to view people as either good or evil, instead of everyone being good and evil. People on the political left believe they are the holders of truth while the other side is evil. People on the political right believe the exact opposite. The story that each side might be both is a story that is simply unacceptable. There is no memetic priming for that story. There is no such story, and there are no such storytellers.

True truths are versions for which there is no demand in a world of fake truths. That's a sign of the truth.

---

147. If we accept the existence of duality—the coexistence of "good" and "evil" in ourselves and every human being—then the story of Genesis would rewrite itself. For each of us to always simultaneously harbor "good" and "evil" within us, our progenitors would be rewritten to be Eve and the serpent instead of the popular version in which our progenitors were written to be Adam and Eve. That small change could be said to be the shell game played by the story itself, and by the storytellers, looking to sell and promote the latter, mutated version of the story. The former version is less appealing to an audience and won't sell. The marketplace for popular stories selects the most commodified versions of the original story.

Final Word

"The Man" is a colloquial phrase that refers to the systemic oppression of individuals by forces such as globalization, commercialization, big business, and government.[148] "Stick it to The Man" is an idiomatic expression of defiance against these forces of oppression.[149] The moniker can be seen as a modern way to describe a self-expanding tyrannical system, which we have referred to in this book as a "beast." The next step in the evolution of this thinking is to realize that The Man is actually Us.[150]

To date, no act of defiance against The Man has gained more traction than the annual ritual known as Burning Man, which has taken burning an effigy to an unprecedented level of spectacle. It's not meant to be a perfect expression of the counterculture to all that is oppressing people. Nothing can be. Burning Man nonetheless remains the most intriguing attempt to break the oligopoly that self-expanding beasts have on culture and the human experience.

It is perhaps appropriate, then, to close this book with a story about Burning Man.

"Welcome home." What a strange thing to say to someone you've just met, I thought. Plus, this was not my idea of home. This was actually just about the opposite of my idea of home—the shelter I had left behind eight hours earlier that had suburban comforts such as copper plumbing and air conditioning. It was the end of summer, and I was on my way to attend my first Burning Man,

---

148. See https://www.allwords.com/word-stick+it+to+the+man.html; https://www.etymonline.com/word/man.
149. See https://www.allwords.com/word-stick+it+to+the+man.html.
150. The majority of us burning the effigy of The Man at Burning Man actually contribute to the exact system we rail against as being The Man.

an annual performance art of 70,000 volunteer refugees hauling one complete Walmart Supercenter to an evaporated lake bed.[151]

Like most normal people, of course, I had resisted years of beckoning by people I otherwise consider friends to come to this blighted place—a Habitat Not for Humanity. The more pictures they showed and stories they told, the less interested I had become. In the photos, the place looked like Pompeii just as the dust was settling. Not exactly central Pompeii, but perhaps a lesser known trailer park near Pompeii. The people in the photos were frozen in poses and expressions that suggested they did not have time to put on their clothes when calamity struck.

Finally, one of them had said, "Forget all the photos and stories. If you trust me, you should join us." A beautiful paean to friendship. Or possibly how the Devil pitched Faust. I'm sure the Devil (playa name: Angel) would identify with being a "burner," and I like bargains. In the broader context, a new millennium was about to dawn, and I was running out of excuses. So I had told them, in a tone of resignation, that I would join them. But only if I could drive my own getaway car.

———————————

At this point, I have not rolled down my window yet. There is no rush when you might be at the Gates of Hell.[152] Alas, I am in the middle of a dust hurricane, and—in a moment of cash register impulsiveness—I had upgraded my Ducky's car wash to include upholstery vacuuming two days earlier. She tapped on the driver's side window: "Please open your trunk." That was the other reason I hadn't rolled down my window yet. If I were to describe the person I would want to welcome me home after a long trip, she was not it. Not even the lingerie part.

This particular lingerie model was sporting blue ski goggles (Walmart, $19.99). Keep in mind that I had just crossed into a flat desert inferno from

151. Also one-half of a 747, since 2016.
152. If camping downwind of gases fuming from a row of 22 Port-A-Potties, which turn into fertilizer greenhouses in the baking sun, is not Hell, then I don't know what is.

Wadsworth, Nevada, which itself is a desert town.[153] There was no Alpine ski hill in sight. What was really out of place, however, were the two gold cones with pointy tips protruding over her mammary glands. I decided to put on protective goggles of my own before rolling down the window.

"Please open your trunk," she requested again. Thank God, a mark of civilization. She's apparently going to take my luggage to my room, I thought. I really hadn't given this Burning Man festival enough benefit of the doubt. I was ready to tip a lot because in the trunk of my car I had packed enough stuff to run away and start a new life in Mexico. And just what would you bring if you were starting a new life in Mexico? Certainly a lot less than what I packed for a few days' sleepaway at Burning Man.[154]

The thought did cross my mind that she might not be the world's most partially dressed bellhop. If not the bellhop, who was she? What did this begoggled lingerie model want? Only years later would I learn that she was a border patrol agent screening for drugs and stowaways accompanying millionaires who were leaving the American Dream in search of a refugee encampment. In my jeans and pressed shirt (Walmart, $47.06 total), I probably didn't look like the rest of the volunteer laborers they needed in Burning Man nation to build semi-stable dwellings for this Habitat Not for Humanity. Looking back at that customs moment, we were probably sizing each other up.

What I do recall about that moment is that she wasn't wearing much except a smile, as they say, but I wouldn't have known if she was smiling because her face was covered with a bandana (Walmart, $2.99) to the point of being incognito. Again, only years later would I come to understand that ambivalence is not an uncommon feature of Burning Man performance art. For the time being, however, it was hard to tell if I was about to get a bikini car wash or be

153. The town is deserted, but I repeat myself.
154. For Mexico, I would just need some cash and a sense of adventure. At Burning Man, the latter will get you far but the former won't. U.S. currency is not accepted anywhere on the playa, except to purchase three things: coffee, ice, and iced coffee.

carjacked and stuffed in the trunk. Anything seemed possible, and because of that, for the second time that day, prudence suggested I turn around and drive back to San Francisco.

San Francisco was founded on June 29, 1776, by colonists from Spain. Elsewhere that same week, a committee of five colonists far to the East drafted—while wearing wigs and costumes—divorce papers from the establishment to birth a new kind of experimental civilization. Some of the drafters went on to clarify what they meant a few years later by writing up the ten basic principles.[155] They couldn't quite stop there and kept adding more to the list. Eventually, some people decided they needed a less federal and more feral environment. They piled all their belongings onto cobbled-together vehicles and headed off on a dusty trek in search of a different kind of culture.

In the beginning of the 19th century, San Francisco would have qualified as a wild place. Wild, as in there was nothing there. You couldn't fault anyone for not wanting to build a city on a fault. Then James Marshall announced that there were what looked like bits of coins in the American River in 1848, and suddenly entrepreneurs from all over upended their lives to rush to the region and mine this particular alternative to the U.S. dollar.

San Francisco incorporated itself in 1850 to accommodate this influx of unwashed entrepreneurs. Stories from those early years suggest it was a bit of a free-for-all: an eclectic, random mix of adventurers from all walks of life trying to build a city from scratch in a short period of time. Free-for-all, in this case, doesn't mean it was a gift economy; it meant everything possible was for

---

155. See https://en.wikipedia.org/wiki/United_States_Bill_of_Rights.

sale—picks, shovels, women, drugs, and dreams. To apparel this emerging class of hedonists, a cottage industry arose to make revolutionary clothing the world had never seen before: the aforementioned jeans. An epicenter of Wild West mayhem was born.

A New Yorker friend once threw down the following gauntlet: between her home city and San Francisco, which had contributed more to revolutionary culture?

There is no contest. San Francisco spawned the computing revolution, the hippie revolution, the venture capital revolution, the gay revolution, the biotech revolution, the Internet revolution, the revolutionary idea that young people can start companies, the social media revolution, and the Blockchain revolution. All of these phenomena have gone global. During the same span, what phenomenon that germinated in NYC has gone global? Ok, I'm not being fair. The financial crisis did start in NYC.

To be even fairer, many of the great revolutions birthed in San Francisco were started by people who were being shunned by a semi-tolerant Bay Area culture. Burning Man is an example. If it hadn't been for a city cop telling Larry Harvey to take his Baker Beach fire hazard on the road, he never would have discovered Black Rock City.

Black Rock City is not the kind of place you would have discovered on your own.[156] Not surprisingly, the federal government—an institution that comes to

---

156. If you type "Black Rock City" into Google Maps, the search engine thinks it is near Blowfish Sushi. A blowfish, incidentally, is an aquatic beast known not only for being poisonous but for its artistic talents. Despite some of David Best's better attempts at building temples using complex geometric designs at Burning Man, David Attenborough has called the Blowfish "the greatest artist of the animal kingdom," due to the males' unique habit of wooing females by creating nests in sand composed of complex geometric designs, according to a direct quote from Wikipedia. Also, in case you were wondering, Blowfish Sushi, which relies on precision knifing to protect patrons, so far has maimed no more diners than Benihana.

mind for some people when they think of "The Man"—directed Larry and his group of wayward libertarians to a location that would be difficult to find and was devoid of livability to create his experimental civilization.[157]

To get to Black Rock City—a fictional address in the mold of John Steinbeck's Eden—you first have to head east on Highway 80 from Reno. It becomes quickly clear, extrapolating from early numbers, that you will see less than ten living creatures over the next seven hundred miles. The utter barrenness has a way of bringing out the worst of one's neuroses. If I blow a tire and careen into a ditch, how many years until someone finds my remains? Are those vultures I see ahead or floaters in my eye? How many unreported in-laws did the Donner party have to dismember for food during this vast desert crossing before getting stuck at the pass for the winter?

Fortunately, before the mind can wander too far down this road of grizzly desperation, you are asked by the Burning Man manual to make a 90 degree left turn off the freeway. That's correct: drive perpendicularly away from your last connection to modern infrastructure toward a minimalist horizon. Within minutes you are without cell reception, GPS signal, or your previous courage about this whole undertaking.

The hours pass. In the totally blank desert, you are searching for a town called Empire to fuel up, and when you get there you realize it is an empire about the size of a gas station and everyone has no clothes. At this point, the Burning Man manual tells you that you have farther to go to get to the gates of Black Rock City. Parched, increasingly delirious, and self-conscious about having overdressed for the occasion, for the first time I wondered if I should turn around.

---

157. The federal government hosting the burning of an effigy of itself would be akin to King George III hosting a wild party for the signing of the Declaration of Independence.

Had I turned around then, or later at what I thought were the Gates of Hell, I wouldn't have been able to close this book with this final thought.

Human endeavor creates value. It is what we support through our foundation. It is what builds beautiful things and what solves problems. It is the basis of our faith that humans will eventually, at some distant time, solve everything—whatever that means. We're going to go out on a limb and say that the time horizon for this happening is ten thousand years, which is a way of saying—like that final drive into the desert—we have no idea how long this voyage will actually take.

A more interesting question than "when" is "what." What will we do after we solve everything—including longevity, space travel, world peace, and interdependent stakeholding? We will probably do then exactly what we had been doing until approximately ten thousand years ago: gather around the fire, tell stories, and dance. This is what we have done since the beginning of time and will do until the end of time. It's the enduring human story that stretches in both directions outside the current 20,000-year Grand Interlude—the only strange epoch in human history where we got caught up in the belly of the beast. Will life be dull thereafter? Hardly. There will always be the love story, and that story never ends.

Of course, we are about as aware of living in the Grand Interlude as fish are aware of living in water. The Grand Interlude is all we've ever known, so we think this is normal. Burning Man, then, is that rare glimpse into the timeless, inaccessible life outside of the Grand Interlude. If you haven't gone yet, I'm not going to tell you stories about it, or tell you to trust me. But I will tell you this. Being in this otherworldly place called Burning Man will feel like being home. Sublimely. Now close your eyes and imagine what it means to go home to a place you've never been.

Welcome home.

ABOUT THE AUTHORS

DR. JOON YUN is President of Palo Alto Investors LP, a hedge fund founded in 1989. Board certified in radiology, Joon served on the clinical faculty at Stanford. Joon is a trustee of the Salk Institute and was the $2 million founding donor to the National Academy of Medicine Aging and Longevity Grand Challenge. Joon holds a MD from Duke Medical School and a BA from Harvard University. He has been to Burning Man the past 19 years.

JEREMY YUN is Director of Yun Family Foundation. He is also a guitarist, songwriter, and co-founder of the band WJM. With his band, Jeremy has appeared live in front of millions of viewers on prime time TV shows such as NBC's *Little Big Shots* and the European TV show *Super Kids*. He and his bandmates have performed at rock festivals, the United Nations, Burning Man, YouTube, the Leukemia and Lymphoma Society, and UCSF Benioff Children's Hospital. Jeremy gave a TEDx talk "The New Social Contract" in 2017 and serves on the board of the Purpose Awards.

CONRAD YUN has over 20 years of experience as an investor and entrepreneur. Conrad manages a family office with investments across a range of public and private assets, including in numerous startups. Conrad is also Executive Director of Yun Family Foundation and its affiliate Palo Alto Institute, which are nonprofits sponsoring initiatives in the areas of aging, nutrition, childhood diseases, technology and art. Previously, Conrad worked in the technology sector as an executive and founder of startups in Europe and Asia and also as a corporate lawyer at Cravath, Swaine & Moore. Conrad is a CFA charterholder and holds a JD from University of Chicago Law School and a BA from Harvard University.